MAR 2 4 2006

Property of Kalmbach Publishing Co.
Library

U.S. Navy PB4Y-1 (B-24) Liberator Squadrons

D0879369

U.S. Navy

PB4Y-1 (B-24) Liberator Squadrons in Great Britain during World War II

Alan C. Carey

Schiffer Military History
Atglen, PA

Acknowledgments

Special thanks to Gene S. McIntyre, Fleet Air Wing Seven (FAW-7) Historian and veteran of VB-103, and Mike Jarrett for providing me with a considerable amount of information for this book. Mr. McIntyre provided me with a wealth of personal stories written by veterans and printed in his Fleet Air Wing Seven News-letters; the VB-110 photo album of Rear Admiral James Reedy, individual photographs, and contacts. Mr. Jarrett provided me with hundreds of photographs from the Dunkeswell Memorial Museum, official and unofficial documents on FAW-7 (Fleet Air Wing Seven) Liberator operations, statistics, and information from his published and unpublished works on the men of Dunkeswell and Upottery. I also would like to thank all the veterans and their families for contributing material to Gene McIntyre, Mike Jarrett, and myself.

Alan C. Carey
June 2002

Book Design by Ian Robertson.

Copyright © 2003 by Alan C. Carey.
Library of Congress Catalog Number: 2002116679

All rights reserved. No part of this work may be reproduced or used in any form or by any means—graphic, electronic, or mechanical, including photocopying or information storage and retrieval systems—without written permission from the publisher.

The scanning, uploading and distribution of this book or any part thereof via the Internet or via any other means without the permission of the publisher is illegal and punishable by law. Please purchase only authorized editions and do not participate in or encourage the electronic piracy of copyrighted materials.

"Schiffer," "Schiffer Publishing Ltd. & Design," and the "Design of pen and ink well" are registered trademarks of Schiffer Publishing Ltd.

Printed in China.
ISBN: 0-7643-1775-X

We are interested in hearing from authors with book ideas on related topics.

Published by Schiffer Publishing Ltd.
4880 Lower Valley Road
Atglen, PA 19310
Phone: (610) 593-1777
FAX: (610) 593-2002
E-mail: Info@schifferbooks.com.
Visit our web site at: www.schifferbooks.com
Please write for a free catalog.
This book may be purchased from the publisher.
Please include $3.95 postage.
Try your bookstore first.

In Europe, Schiffer books are distributed by:
Bushwood Books
6 Marksbury Avenue
Kew Gardens
Surrey TW9 4JF
England
Phone: 44 (0) 20 8392-8585
FAX: 44 (0) 20 8392-9876
E-mail: Bushwd@aol.com.
Free postage in the UK. Europe: air mail at cost.
Try your bookstore first.

Contents

Foreword by Gene S. McIntyre

When you have reached the 85-year mark, you have a tendency to look back on your life. This happens on many early mornings when sleep eludes you. You think on many high points, and even a few low ones.

One morning, I started thinking of my many friends that I have in Fleet Air Wing Seven, and how grateful I was for their warm friendship. I therefore must rate FAW-7 as one of the highest points in my life, since it exposed me to great risks. Such risks naturally hones the senses to an extremely fine point that normal life does not. Just ask any man that has traveled in "Harms Way."

I romanticized the likes of my compatriots to the likes of King Arthur's Round Table. All of this coming of course at a much later date in history and a much broader scale in the times existing. Yet, it none the less gave me the feeling of that age. "One for all and all for one." My knights "shipmates" were members of the FAW-7 Round Table. I knew I could depend on them, and they knew that they could depend on me.

When I met many of my knights 55 years later, though they were balding, graying knights of the FAW-7 Round Table, I had a warm, close feeling that the camaraderie of old was still there. For here were friends that, if I needed them, all I had to do was to call and know they would be at my side.

Some later day historian called us "The Greatest Generation" and I cannot refute this, in fact, I heartily endorse this thought when I think back of the several hundred that I have had personal contact. I would ask each of them to come stand by me again with no fear that I would not be able to rely on any one of them. In fact, I would be extremely proud to have them still by my side.

Patriotism, pride in our knights, makes me realize that I have been very fortunate to have served with "The Greatest Generation" and to be apart of the FAW-7 Round Table.

Yes, I can truly say that FAW-7 Round Table has been the high point in my life. I salute you my knights one and all. I am proud that you are a part of my life. God bless each and every one of you.

Gene S. McIntyre
ACOM VB-103 Crew 5
"Plank Owner"
April 2002

Introduction

Many returned home, some stayed forever, none will be forgotten.
-Bernard Stevens, Dunkeswell Historian

Bernard Stevens' tribute characterizes the men of U.S. Navy Fleet Air Wing Seven (FAW-7) who flew the Consolidated B-24 Liberator bomber, the Navy called it the PB4Y-1, from airfields at Dunkeswell and Upottery, England during World War II. Between August 1943 and May 1945, seven PB4Y-1 squadrons consisting of VB/VPB-103, 105, 107, 110, 111, 112, and 114, served in Great Britain. However, only squadrons 103, 105 and 110 served continuously from Dunkeswell. VPB-107 appeared in Britain in January 1945 after completing a very successful tour flying antisubmarine patrols out of Brazil while VB-111 served in England for only a few weeks in October 1943 before transferring to North Africa to join her sister squadrons 112 and 114. The latter squadron, VB-114, operated a detachment of six PB4Y-1s from Dunkeswell between June 1944 and February 1945. VPB-107 and 112 were the last squadrons assigned antisubmarine duty with FAW-7 and were stationed at a nearby U.S. Naval Satellite Field at Upottery.

The Men of Mudville Heights

The United States Navy PB4Y-1 Liberator squadrons stationed in England were unlike their counterparts in the 8th Air Force, who battled their way through thick flak and swarms of German fighters while flying to and from targets over continental Europe. Most of the time, Navy aircrews fought battles of boredom and fatigue while flying 12-hour patrols over the Bay of Biscay and the English Channel.

The job of U.S. Navy aircrews was to keep German U-boats from successfully operating in the Bay of Biscay and the English Channel by going out day after day, often in miserable weather conditions, on unrelenting search and destroy missions. They were young men, the average age was 23, many couldn't legally buy a beer, and most had never been out of their home state. The commanding officers of Navy Liberator squadrons, each responsible for over 200 men and 15 aircraft, were all in their mid-thirties while

Patrol Plane Commanders (PPC), with the job of commanding a 60,000 pound aircraft and 10 to 12 men, were in their early to mid twenties. Likewise, the German men hidden inside U-boats and serving their country were also young, but they had a different type of mission. Their job was to starve the United Kingdom into submission by prohibiting war materials and personnel from reaching the island nation. The U-boat's quest was to hunt down and destroy Allied shipping, while the mission of the Navy planes was to stop them. It was a game of cat and mouse with U.S. Navy PB4Y-1s and U-boats searching for victims and both equal in their own area of expertise in waging war. Both relied on stealth to catch their quarry in a vulnerable position and both invented new methods to improve their chances for success. During the war, FAW-7 Liberators were

Cruising over the English Countryside, PB4Y-1 *Calvert & Coke* "C" B-3 (Navy BurAer 32032). She belonged to VB-103 and arrived at Dunkeswell in September 1943. She was lost in action along with Lt. Ralph Brownell and his crew on 12 November 1943 (Courtesy of Dunkeswell Memorial Museum).

NAVAL AIRCREWMAN'S CREED

I am a United States Naval Aircrewman, member of a combat team. My pilot and shipmates place their trust in me and my guns. I will care for my plane and guns as I care for my life. In them I hold a power of life and death—life for my countrymen, death for the enemy.

I will uphold my trust by protecting my pilot and plane to the absolute limit of my ability.

So help me God.

The Navy Airman's Creed (Courtesy of the Dunkeswell Memorial Museum).

The village of Dunkeswell, Devon, England as it was between 1943-45 (Courtesy of the Dunkeswell Memorial Museum).

responsible for the sinking of five U-boats and damaging many more. However, the men of Dunkeswell paid a heavy price for keeping the U-boat menace in check.

Between 1943 and 1945, nearly 200 Navy Liberator personnel serving with FAW-7 were killed in either operational accidents or in combat. Death often came quickly for a PB4Y-1 Liberator crew. On several occasions, while taking off, landing, or returning to base, a Liberator would slam into the ground with a full load of fuel and bombs, disintegrating in a colossal ball of fire and sending fragments of the plane and its occupants across the ground.

Antisubmarine patrols typically required the aircraft to fly at altitudes ranging from 800 to 1,000 feet as the onboard radar and the eyes of the aircrew scanned the waters below for signs of the enemy. Therefore, flying a PB4Y-1 at such low altitudes placed the 10 to 12 men on board in a highly vulnerable position. Mortal damage to the plane caused by enemy fighters or accurate anti-aircraft fire from a U-boat's crew didn't give a Liberator's crew much of a chance to bail out or radio for help as their stricken bird plummeted towards the sea. The mystery surrounding the disappearance of such aircraft were often solved when an oil slick and pieces of wreckage were spotted on the water's surface. Bodies were hardly ever retrieved; they remain eternally entombed in the Liberator's twisted wreckage lying on the floor of the Bay of Biscay or the English Channel. For the lucky ones who survived, after an aircrew completed 30 missions, they went back to the United States for a 30-day leave before being reassigned. With victory in May 1945, the men rejoined civilian life or continued with military service followed by marriage, children, grandchildren, and great grandchildren.

The Airbase at Dunkeswell

American military personnel referred to Dunkeswell Airfield as "Mudville Heights," in reference to the muddy and wet conditions

that greeted them during the long winter months. Built by civilian contractor George Wimpy between 1941 and 1942, it was originally intended for the Royal Air Force's (R.A.F.) No. 10 Group of Fighter Command but, as the war progressed, the airfield was turned over to British Coastal Command for operations against German submarines.

Beginning in the summer of 1943, three squadrons of United States Army Air Force (U.S.A.A.F.) B-24s operated maritime patrols from the airfield, however, within a month, the U.S. Navy began operations from Dunkeswell. Between 1943 and 1945, the airfield grew in size and, at its peak, more than 5,000 personnel

The hilly roadway at Dunkeswell between the base's living quarters and the hangars/runway. The telephone box (center left) outside the thatched Dunkeswell Post Office was used by military personnel (Courtesy of Harry Ross via Dunkeswell Memorial Museum).

were stationed at the base. In March 1944, the station became a United States Navy Air Facility (U.S.N.A.F.), an upgrade giving it a unique position of being the only United States Navy Air Station in the entire European Theater of Operations.

Dunkeswell was a serene little village of a few hundred inhabitants when the Americans arrived in the summer of 1943 bringing with them excitement and change to the little rural hamlet, especially for the children. One of them, Bernard Stevens, as a young boy, lived on nearby Lower Northcott Farm, which was located within a half mile from where the bombers parked (called hardstands). He, sometimes his older brother, and other children would watch day after day and marvel as the mammoth, four-engine PB4Y-1 Liberators lifted off the ground to begin the hunt for German U-boats. After the war, Stevens' devotion to the American flyers never wavered as he and other local citizenry struggled to insure that the memory of the American presence at Dunkeswell wouldn't be forgotten. Almost a half century later, Stevens became a curator and historian for the Dunkeswell Memorial Museum; a facility devoted to preserving the history of Navy Liberator squadrons that served at the airfield.

After the Second World War, the villagers wouldn't forget the sacrifices or the impression the Navy airmen made upon them in their common struggle against an often-brutal enemy. In 1962, a local news article featured a story about Mrs. Driver, a local woman whom the American sailors called "Granny Driver." She said, "There was never a day when I didn't have someone in here. The officers used to come in and ask if I could cook dinner for so many. I cooked geese and chicken for them." One U.S. serviceman, Joe Spalding, spent a great deal of time at 'Granny Driver's' and would anxiously scan the night sky outside the cottage for Liberators, which had not returned from missions."[1]

The villagers provided something, maybe more important in psychological terms to the young Americans—open homes and open hearts to young men far from home. The American's in return provided luxury items the local townspeople hadn't seen in years or never at all from Pineapple juice to ice cream and base personnel also held Christmas parties for local children.

This is the story of those men who served at Dunkeswell, and the neighboring satellite airfield at Upottery, which, as Bernard Stevens eloquently stated in his description, "*Many returned home, some stayed forever, none will be forgotten.*" The men of FAW-7 will never be forgotten.

Aerial view of Dunkeswell Airfield taken in 1943 (Courtesy of the Dunkeswell Memorial Museum).

The Consolidated B-24/PB4Y-1 Liberator

Take-offs in a B-24 were the most sweated times especially when loaded with bombs and 2700 gallons of high-octane gasoline. The bump of the crossing runway at Dunkeswell we felt was the commit point and all eyes in the after station would be on the wing and wheels.

-Charles Lindstedt, Crew 10, VB-105,
October 1943-July 1944.

The Consolidated B-24 Liberator was a tool of war, designed to deliver bombs on enemy targets. In historical terms, the B-24 Liberator is the less glamorous American bomber of World War II. That distinction goes to the Boeing Company's B-17 Flying Fortress. As for the Liberator, you either loved it or loathed it, especially for those who wanted to fly the B-17. The following poem written by an unknown author highlights the feelings towards the aircraft:

For there's a sort of maniac madness in the supercharger's whine,
as you hear the ice cubes tinkling in the turbo balance lines.
and the runway strips are narrow, but the snowbanks, they are wide,
While the crash trucks say, in a mournful way, that you're on that final ride.
The nose gear rocks and trembles, for it's held with baling wire,
and the wings are filled with thermite to make a hotter fire.
The camouflage is peeling off; it lends an added lustre,
while each pitot head is filled with lead to help the load adjuster.
The bomb-bay doors are rusted, and close with a ghastly shriek,
and the plexi-glass is smeared with some forgotten oil leak.
The oleo strut struts are twisted; the wheels are not quite round,
and the bulkheads thin (Ford builds with tin) emit a wrenching sound.
You taxi out to the runway, 'mid the groans of the tortured gear
and you feel the check-rider's teeth gnawing at your tender rear.
The co-pilot dozing on the right, in a liquor laden coma
mingles his breath, like the kiss of death, with the putt-putt's foul aroma.
So it's off in the overcast yonder, though number one is missing,
and the hydraulic fluid escaping sets up a gentle hissing.
the compass dial is spinning in a way that brooks no stopping
and row by row the fuses blow with an intermittent popping.
It was named the "Liberator" by a low and twisted mind,
but the men, who come to Liberal, no freedom ever find.
there is no hope no sunny ray, to dry their tears of sorrow,
for those who land and still can stand, must fly again tomorrow.

Close-up view of No. 8 *Wild Her*, a Fleet Air Wing 7 Liberator (Courtesy of the Dunkeswell Memorial Museum).

Side profile of Liberator "O." Note fire extinguishers in the foreground (Courtesy of the Dunkeswell Memorial Museum).

B-6 "T" of VB-105 making her final approach to Dunkeswell. This plane has the Emerson nose turret rather than the preferred ERCO turret (Courtesy of the Dunkeswell Memorial Museum).

PB4Y-1 "U" (BuAer 63924) of VB-105 being fueled on 10th September 1944 (Courtesy of the Dunkeswell Memorial Museum).

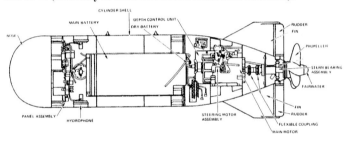

Diagram for the *Fido/Zombie* Mark-24 Aerial Mine that was used by FAW-7 aircraft. Weight: 308 kg /680 1bs. Length: 2134mm /7ft 0in . Range: 3660m /4000yds at 12 knots. Explosive Charge: 42 kg /92 1bs Torpex (Courtesy of the Dunkeswell Memorial Museum).

Dunkeswell living quarters of Lt. George Poulos who was a Patrol Plane Commander with VB-103. The officers are Ensign Burness, Lt. Thompson, Lt. George Poulos, Lt. Commander Von Brecht, and Commanding Officer of VB-103, Lt. Kempe, Lt. Peterson, and Lt. (jg) Lieutenant Sivers (sp). Lt. Bruce Morgan who went on to become a Hollywood stuntman took the picture (Courtesy of George Poulos via Dunkeswell Memorial Museum)

With a length of 67 feet, a wingspan of 110 feet, and a gross weight of 60,000 pounds, The Liberator was an imposing monster for the time. Powered by four Pratt and Whitney R-1830-43/65 engines, it had a top speed of 279 miles per hour, a service ceiling of 31,000 feet and a range of 2,960 miles. For delivering the war to the enemy, it could carry a maximum bomb load of 8,800 pounds and defend itself with ten Browning 50-caliber machine guns. It was a tool of war and, as a veteran described, "It was always cold in those planes. Creature comforts were not part of the aircraft's design."[2]

It was built for the Army Air Force, yet the Navy acquired it to fulfill the need for a long-range patrol plane. Other Navy patrol aircraft, such as the Consolidated PBY-5 Catalina, the Martin Mariner PBM, and the Consolidated PB2Y were too slow and lightly armed. The Navy wanted the B-24 while the United States Army Air Force needed a manufacturing facility to build the B-29 Superfortress. Hence, in July 1942, the Navy agreed to cancel the PBB-1 Sea Ranger seaplane being built at the Boeing plant in Renton, Washington in exchange for a quantity of B-24 Liberators. The Navy designated the B-24 as the PB4Y-1. The squadrons es-

Mark-24 *Zombie* inside a bomb bay. A United States Navy patrol plane of VP-84 made the first U-boat kill with a Mk-24 on 14 May 1943 (Courtesy of the Dunkeswell Memorial Museum).

A Mark-24 *Zombie* hitting the water after being released from a PB4Y-1 (Courtesy of the Dunkeswell Memorial Museum).

B-12 "M" *Piccadilly Pam* (BuAer 90474) in all her splendor. Note the APS-15 search radar that replaced the Sperry belly turret. Like many aircraft after the war, *Piccadilly Pam* came to an inglorious end when she was scrapped at Stillwater, Oklahoma (Courtesy of the Dunkeswell Memorial Museum).

A Mark-24 Safety Poster (Courtesy of the Dunkeswell Memorial Museum).

tablished were designated VB for Navy Bombing until 1 October 1944 when the designation was changed to VPB for Navy Patrol Bomber.

In the Pacific War, Navy Liberators, and later its sister, the Consolidated-Vultee PB4Y-2 Privateer, made it possible to cover wider search sectors than before, conduct offensive strikes against enemy ground installations, shipping and, more importantly, provide extensive photographic reconnaissance before a major operation. In the European Theater, it was used primarily for antisubmarine warfare (ASW).

The first Navy Liberators varied little from the Army B-24D with the distinctive Plexiglas nose with free-hand machine guns mounted to protect against frontal attacks by enemy fighters. The distinctive Navy version of the Liberator was introduced with the introduction of the ERCO (Engineering and Research Company) bow turret that extended the length of the aircraft by three feet. The bow turret had twin .50-caliber guns and carried twice the ammunition supply of other turrets-800 versus 400. However, some PB4Y-1s retained the Consolidated A-6A/B or Emerson A-15 nose turrets. In addition, because Navy Liberators were to operate a considerable amount of time over water, state-of-the-art electronics and navigational gear were installed such as the APS-15 search radar, which replaced the Sperry belly turret, the AN/ARC-1 radar intercept receiver, and LORAN. A total of 977 PB4Y-1 Liberators (the majority being D and J models) were received by the Navy before the end of World War II. Approximately 200 of them found their way to England between August 1943 and May 1945.

Flying the PB4Y-1
According to George F. Poulos, a Patrol Plane Commander with Navy Squadron VB-103, the PB4Y-1 wasn't an easy plane to fly. "It was unstable and very heavy on the controls. When more than nominal aileron application was necessary, the wing tips twisted,

B-7 "U" of VB-105 over the coast of England (Courtesy of the Dunkeswell Memorial Museum).

making it impossible to fly a good formation. At the overloaded conditions we operated under, the Davis wing often twisted, increasing drag to a point where cruise speed would be reduced by 15 percent. For the first four or five hours of a mission, it was often necessary to add power, nose over, regain your speed, your altitude, and reset cruise settings.

The duration of the mission made it necessary to carry fuel in wing and auxiliary tanks. Transfer of fuel to the main tanks were subject to leakage, requiring turning off all electrical and electronic circuits, rendering the mission a impotent during this period. Main-

taining a balanced load of fuel in the four main tanks was always a problem. Near the end of a 12-13 hour long mission you were always alert to the fact one of the engines might be starved even though the total fuel available was adequate." Indeed, a number of PB4Y-1s based in Europe and the Pacific crashed due to fuel starvation.

"The landing gear was weak and subject to staying unlocked in both the up and down positions. Conversely, the nose gear often stayed up and locked when you wanted it down and locked." Again, failure of the nose gear was a common occurrence with the B-24,

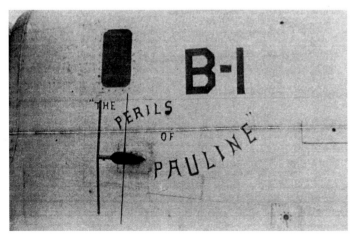

B-1 *Perils of Pauline*. As of this book's publication, the nose art of most Fleet Air Wing 7 PB4Y-1 have not been matched to specific aircraft (Courtesy of the Dunkeswell Memorial Museum).

B-16 *Johnny Boy* of VB/VPB-103 with 15 "V" mission markings (Courtesy of the Dunkeswell Memorial Museum).

VB-103

Mission Symbols V

Aircraft marked B-1 'A'to B-12 'M' (Sept.1943).

VB-105

Mission symbols ★

Aircraft marked B-1 'O', B-2 'P' & etc.

VB-110

●

Mission Symbols

Aircraft marked B-1 'A', B-2 'B', & etc.

Mission and aircraft markings for VB/VPB-103, VB/VPB-105, and VB/VPB-110 (Courtesy of Mike Jarrett).

B-8 *Donna Jean* (Courtesy of the Dunkeswell Memorial Museum).

B-8 *Brooklyn Bombshell* (Courtesy of the Dunkeswell Memorial Museum).

which invariably caused extensive damage upon landing.[3]

The Liberator was difficult to fly, noisy, cold, leaked fuel, and it had a weak front nose gear. Yet, with all its shortcomings, the aircraft could take a considerable amount of punishment and still be able to return home. It was a tool of war built during the 1930's and, by the end of World War II, had grown obsolete. By the late-1940's, only a handful were still in service with the U.S. Navy. Most went straight to the scrap yard after the war and were melted down. However, it served the U.S. Navy's need for a long-range patrol bomber and, in that respect, it proved its worth to British Coastal Command, the U.S. Navy and the men of Fleet War Wing 7.

B-11 *Little Susan* (Courtesy of the Dunkeswell Memorial Museum).

No. 2 *Nite Hop* (Courtesy of the Dunkeswell Memorial Museum).

No. 10 *Lazy May-Z*. Note the absence of machine guns in the nose turret (Courtesy of the Dunkeswell Memorial Museum).

1

The Battle of the Atlantic and the Birth of Fleet Air Wing Seven

The aeroplane can no more eliminate the submarine than a crow can fight a mole.

-Admiral Doenitz, August 1942

On 3 September 1939, four years before the first Navy B-24 Liberator touched down on the concrete runway at Dunkeswell, the Battle of the Atlantic began with the German submarine U-30 sinking the British Ocean liner *Athenia* off the coast of Ireland. This event sparked the beginning of the longest campaign in World War II and it would cost the lives of thousands of sailors, airmen, and merchant mariners.

With the fall of France in June 1940, Britain stood alone against the might of Germany's air and sea power. Hitler's ultimate goal was to starve Britain into submission by mounting a naval blockade to stop war materials and food supplies from reaching the island nation. Germany's primary weapon the U-boat, operating in Wolf-packs of up to a dozen or more vessels, hunted merchant ships trying to make their way across the Atlantic from North and South America. For mutual protection, the ships formed convoys protected by a screen of British destroyers yet, this couldn't stop the U-boats unrelenting attacks, and losses mounted to the point that it was very doubtful Britain could survive.

By September 1941, three months before the United States entered the war, the United States Navy began the dangerous game of escorting convoys on their journey to Britain, which put American lives in harms way. It was only a matter of time before American servicemen and civilians became casualties of an undeclared war. On 15 October, the American destroyer U.S.S. *Kearny*, while escorting a 50-ship convoy, was torpedoed and damaged by U-568, claiming the lives of 11 sailors. A couple of weeks later two more American ships, the merchantman U.S.S. *LeHigh* and the destroyer U.S.S. *Reuben James*, were sunk and over 100 men were lost.[4]

New Tactics and Weapons

To meet the challenges of fighting the Battle of the Atlantic, the British and Americans formulated antisubmarine tactics using new weapons such as the hedgehog depth charge, underwater detection

Vice Admiral Arthur L. Bristol, Commanding Officer of Task Force 24, and the namesake of Bristol Field, Argentia, Newfoundland (Courtesy of U.S. Navy).

A snowplow clears a runway at Bristol Field where VB-103 originally operated. This was the type of weather often encountered by Fleet Air Wing 7 aircraft while stationed at Argentia (Courtesy of U.S. Navy).

Fleet Admiral Ernest J. King meeting with FAW-7 staff. The officer on the right is Commander Thomas Durfee, Commander U.S. Naval Facility (NAF), Dunkeswell. In the background is Admiral Stark's Lodestar. Admiral Stark was the Commander-in-Chief, U.S. 12th Fleet (Courtesy of the Dunkeswell Memorial Museum).

devices, aerial torpedoes, and airborne radar. These weapons began taking a toll on U-boats especially when German naval codes were broken by British Intelligence. In May 1943 alone, 41 U-boats were sunk; a number surpassing the total losses suffered between 1939 and 1940. Oblivious to the fact that their codes had been broken, the German Navy continued to send submarines and their crews out to sea in an effort to stem the flow of Allied war materials to Europe.

Two new antisubmarine weapons developed by the United States between 1942 and 1943 played important roles during the Battle of the Atlantic and with Fleet Air Wing Seven aircraft-the AN/CRT-1 Sonobouy and the Mark-24 Acoustical Aerial Mine. Both were the latest in antisubmarine warfare and worked on the principle of passive acoustics. Since radar couldn't detect a submerged submarine, the sonobouy was introduced. About 5 inches in diameter and 4 feet long, the AN/CRT-1 held a hydrophone attached to a 30-foot wire, which was released upon impact with the water. A radio operator on board a patrol plane would then listen for sounds emanating from a submarine's screws. However, it had one major flaw. A single bouy couldn't give a precise location of a target; therefore, a pattern of bouys would be sowed in an effort to pinpoint the submarine's location. Once a German submarine was detected, the aircraft would then initiate a bombing run with depth charges and/or Mark-24 Aerial Mines.

The Mark-24 Aerial Mine, called the *Zombie* by the British and U.S. Navy Air Forces in Britain, was in actuality an aerial torpedo, which could detect and home in on the cavitation noise of a submarine's screws. In the fall of 1941, the U.S. Navy asked the Office of Scientific Research and Development (OSRD) for a fea-

Commodore William Hamilton, Commander-in-Chief, Fleet Air Wing 7 (Courtesy of the Dunkeswell Memorial Museum).

Commodore Hamilton welcoming Admiral King as he arrives at Dunkeswell on 16 June 1944 (Courtesy of the Dunkeswell Memorial Museum).

Admiral King meets with staff at Dunkeswell on 16 June 1944. On the left is Lt. Commander James Reedy, Commanding Officer VB-110. In the background behind Commodore Hamilton is G. C. Miller, Commanding Officer, Naval Air Station Dunkeswell (Courtesy of the Dunkeswell Memorial Museum).

One of the original VB-103 crews to serve in England was Lt. Gale Burkey and Crew 5. Top row (left to right): R. F. "Frenchy" LeClair (ARM1c), Ensign Teague (co-pilot), Gail C. Burkey (PPC) Ensign "Dutch" Dehaan (navigator), Lt. Tony Sivo (pilot), and Edward W. Callaway (ARM3c). Bottom row: Yenzer (AOM3c), unknown, Jerry John (AMM1c), Gene S. McIntyre (AOM1c), Eddie Miller (AOM3c), and unknown (Courtesy of Gene McIntyre).

sibility study for developing an acoustic, air-launched, antisubmarine torpedo. On 10 December 1941, the OSRD held a meeting at Harvard University to study the proposal with General Electric, David Taylor Model Basin, the Harvard University Underwater Sound Laboratory, and Bell Laboratories. By March 1943, fifteen months after conception, the Mark-24 went in production. The first U-boat destroyed by the weapon occurred on 14 May 1943 when a PBY Catalina of VP-84 flown by Lt. P.A. Bodinet sank a German submarine southwest of Iceland.[5]

The Birth of Fleet Air Wing-7

By early 1941, Great Britain was losing the Battle of the Atlantic and, with the real prospect of the United States being drawn into the conflict, the U.S. Navy began devising a plan to protect the Atlantic sea lanes. In March 1941, out of this necessity to conduct proper aerial and surface observation of the waters off the eastern seaboard, the U.S. Navy organized the predecessor to Fleet Air Wing-7, Patrol Wing, Support Force, Atlantic Fleet. The establish-

ment of the patrol wing would, two years later, give rise to the first Navy B-24 Liberator squadron to serve in England.

The function of the Patrol Wing was to provide antisubmarine, anti-raider, and shipping protection from Cape Hatteras to Newfoundland (patrols were later extended to Iceland and Greenland). For the next nine months, U.S. Navy Patrol Squadrons (VP) 51, 52, 53, 55, and 56 (equipped with such aircraft as the Consolidated PBY-5 Catalina and Martin PBM flying boat) conducted aerial surveillance, and mapping. These squadrons were based at Quonset Point, Rhode Island, Norfolk, Virginia, and Argentia, Newfoundland.

On 17 May 1941, Fleet Admiral Ernest J. King, Chief of Naval Operations, issued confidential serial 023438 to the commanding officers of the Atlantic and Pacific Fleets, which ordered a reorganization of Patrol Plane Wings. This reorganization split the Support Force into two wings: Patrol Wing 7 and Patrol Wing 8 (the patrol squadrons were then re-numbered as 71, 72, 73, 74, and 81). On 12 September 1941, the Patrol Wing's mission was clarified

El Mundo the Great, **the mascot of Lt. Burkey's crew, who flew with VB-103 (Courtesy of Gene McIntyre).**

Usually reporting for duty with bloodshot eyes, Lt. Richard Quinlan of VB-103 was nicknamed "Beet Eyes." Here he is at the controls of a PB4Y-1 (Courtesy of the Dunkeswell Memorial Museum).

Lt. Gordon Milbrath and Lt. (jg) Hart on top of a VB-103 PB4Y-1 (Courtesy of Gordon Milbrath via Dunkeswell Memorial Museum).

Lt. Charles "Muck" Muckenthaler (left) stands next to his aircraft B-5 "E" *Muck's Mauler*. (BurAer 32035). Standing with him (left to right): J.A. Crossman and Kenneth L. Wright. Note the plane's olive drab upper surfaces and gull gray under surfaces. Later Navy patrol planes adopted the ASW paint scheme of Sea Blue upper surfaces and white/light gray lower surfaces (Courtesy of Craig Ewing).

when Captain Mullinnix, Commanding Officer of the Argentia Air Detachment, issued Operation Plan No. 1-41 (revised on 23 October 1941) which dictated that Wing aircraft would operate in the "Western Atlantic Area." This area, as defined in the FAW-7 War Diary, would be:

"Bounded on the east by a line from the north along 10 degrees west as far south as latitude 53 degrees north. Thence by rhumb line to latitude 53 degrees north, longitude 26 degrees west. Thence south, and extending as far west as the continental land areas but excluding Naval Coastal Frontier, Naval District land and waters areas, Canadian coastal zones, and the territorial waters of Latin American countries."

The Wing's mission within the area would be the following:

Protect United States and foreign flag shipping other than German and Italian against hostile attack by:
1. Escorting, covering, and patrolling for the defense of convoys, and, by destroying German and Italian naval, land, and air forces encountered.
2. Insure the safety of sea communications with U.S. strategic outposts.
3. Support the defense of U.S. territory and bases, Iceland and Greenland.
4. Trail merchant vessels suspected of supplying or otherwise assisting the operations of German or Italian naval vessels or aircraft.

The operations plan stressed that Wing aircraft were to:

MAINTAIN CONSTANT AND IMMEDIATE READINESS TO REPEL HOSTILE ATTACK. OPERATE AS UNDER WAR CONDITION, INCLUDING COMPLETE DARKENING OF PLANES WHEN ON ESCORT DUTY DURING DARKNESS, VARYING PLANE ALTITUDES AS NECESSARY.

Almost two months before Pearl Harbor, the U.S. Navy was on a war footing and prepared to defend American shipping against enemy submarines. The task of Patrol Wing Seven remained constant through the United States entry into the war and into 1943. Patrol squadrons were added or transferred and faster or modified aircraft became available for the Wing's use, the PBO Hudson and the PV-1 Ventura being two examples. In May 1942, Patrol Wing-7s designation changed to Fleet Air Wing 7. Exactly one year later, the Wing's ASW arsenal would be strengthened by the addition of the B-24 Liberator.

Army vs. Navy Antisubmarine Operations
Before the United States officially went to war and through 1943, both U.S. Army Air Force and Navy patrol aircraft conducted ASW operations in the North and South Atlantic. However, the use of heavy bombers in this role was another matter. Some Air Force and Navy officials were not convinced of the usefulness of heavy bombers for offensive ASW and believed they wouldn't achieve significant success in reducing the threat from submarines. Therefore, it was a waste of time to allocate men and materials to such an operation. Still, the Air Force did deploy a couple of B-24 squadrons in late 1942 and early 1943; the 479th and 480th Antisubmarine Groups. The 479th consisting of the 4th, 19th, and 22nd ASW Squadrons were based at St. Eval and Dunkeswell, England between June and November 1943.

By spring 1943, Allied shipping losses through U-boat attacks in the North Atlantic had reached an alarming proportion with some 3,600 ships being sunk that year. In May 1943, Admiral King, es-

The crew of *Muck's Mauler*. Note the Sea Blue and White/Gray ASW coloring has been applied to the plane. Front row (left to right): Lt. Muchenthaler (PPC), Slohoda (radio/radar operator), Pederson (radio operator), and Ensign Joe Powell (bombardier/navigator). Back row (left to right): Varian (ordnanceman), Stockdale (mechanic), and Ensign Williamson (co-pilot). This aircraft was lost while being ferried back to the U.S. by VB-113, killing all 13 men aboard. VB-113 was a training squadron for PB4Y personnel (Courtesy of Craig Ewing).

tablished the 10th U.S. Fleet with a centralized antisubmarine command, which placed both U.S.A.A.F. and U.S.N. aircraft under the control of the Navy. The 10th Fleet, commanded by Rear Admiral Francis S. Low, didn't have one single ship instead, its task was coordinating and directing naval forces in the Battle of the Atlantic by:

1. The destruction of enemy submarines.
2. The protection of Allied shipping in the Eastern, Gulf, and Caribbean Sea Frontiers.
3. The exercise of convoy shipping that are United States responsibilities.
4. The correlation of United States antisubmarine training and material development training.[6]

However, this decision by Admiral King and, more importantly, his interest in establishing Navy heavy bomber squadrons, didn't sit well with General Marshall or the Army Air Force who believed King was working his way into establishing his own strategic bomber force. The allocation of several hundred B-24D's to the Navy in the fall of 1942 for long-range reconnaissance and ASW work didn't help dispel their suspicions.[7]

After a considerable amount of bickering, the Army Air Force agreed to withdraw from antisubmarine operations and let the Navy take over with the proviso that the Navy would keep it's hands off strategic bombing. However, the Navy did establish over a dozen land-based heavy bombing squadrons in the Pacific under the guise that they were patrol and reconnaissance units although they did participate in anti-shipping sweeps and strategic bombing of enemy installations throughout the Pacific Theater.

In May 1943, VB-103 became the first U.S. Navy B-24 squadron to begin antisubmarine operations in the Atlantic Theater. The employment of the B-24 Liberator in Argentia and later, the United Kingdom, along with PV-1 Ventura squadrons stationed in Greenland and Iceland, permitted continuous air cover for convoys from America to Britain. The introduction of long-range aircraft effectively closed down an area known as the "black hole" of the mid-North Atlantic, which was previously beyond the range of Allied aircraft and where U-boats reigned freely.

VB-103
While the Army and Navy were working out their differences in Washington D.C., on the other side of the United States, Navy Bombing Squadron 103 (VB-103) was commissioned on 15 March 1943, at U.S. Naval Auxiliary Air Station, Camp Kearney, San Diego, California and assigned to Fleet Air Wing 14. Led by Lieutenant Commander William Thomas Easton, a majority of squadron officers and enlisted personnel present at the Commissioning Ceremony had been drawn from PBY-5A Patrol Squadrons 11 and 23, which had returned from action in the South Pacific. A number of pilots came to the squadron from the Transition Landplane Unit at Camp Kearney where they transitioned from one type of plane to another while the balance of the complement of aviators who arrived came directly from flight school. Arriving at Camp Kearney, some of the enlisted men, such as Gene McIntyre and Carlton Lillie, were somewhat surprised to find themselves training as B-24 air crewmen.

Gene McIntyre began his Navy flying career in February 1943 as an enlisted Ordnanceman in PBYs. A month later, he was transferred to VB-103 and was somewhat dumbfounded to find himself assigned to such a squadron. "We couldn't visualize why we were

The VB-103 crew of B-13 *Berlin Express*: Lt. Chet Rief (3rd left), Bruce Higgenbothem (2nd left), and J.A. Crossman (right). The rest of the crew consisted of Ensign Crosby (navigator), J. Moore (AMM2c) Montella (AMM2c) Chiarello (AMM3c) Leavitt (ARM2c), Van Doren (ARM2c), Gibson (ARM3c), Offrell (bombardier), and Farrimond (AOM3c). Note: there were 12 men assigned to the crew but only 9 appear in this photograph. This aircraft crashed on 3 December 1943 killing another crew (Courtesy of the Dunkeswell Memorial Museum).

going to B-24s."[8] Carlton Lillie arrived about the same time as McIntyre and his service with VB-103 would include surviving a ditching of his Liberator in the Bay of Biscay, which resulted in the deaths of three crewmen.

At first, squadron personnel believed they were going to the Pacific as training consisted of low-level bombing tactics. Their assumption wasn't without merit. In February 1943, two Navy PB4Y-1 squadrons, VD-3 and VB-101, began reconnaissance and bombing missions against Japanese-held areas in the Solomons, New Ireland, and New Britain. However, before too long, it became apparent that the squadron was slated for antisubmarine warfare in the Atlantic with Argentia, Newfoundland being the first base of operations.

Through March and into April 1943, men were assigned to aircraft and training on the Liberator commenced, followed by aerial gunnery and bombing practice. The typical PB4Y-1 squadron consisted of 15 aircrews and between 12 to 15 aircraft. Each crew was comprised of three commissioned officers and between seven to eight enlisted men. They were a close-nit group of men who served together in a cramped aircraft and common formalities between officer and enlisted, common in the other branches of the Army and Navy, were forgotten once the plane left the ground. While in England, each crew completed a four-day schedule consisting of a mission, followed by a day of rest, a training day, and a day prepping the aircraft before the next mission. Every six weeks, the crew would get a four-day leave.

On 24 April 1943, VB-103 ground crews left by train for Norfolk, Virginia, with the flight crews following when the outfitting and acceptance check of the planes was completed. The ground crews arrived at Norfolk on 28 April and the first three planes led by Lieutenant Commander Easton arrived the following day. However, a change of orders was issued which diverted the squadron to Quonset Point, Rhode Island for two weeks of training consisting of practice antisubmarine flights, use of the APS-15 radar, sonobouys and the top secret Mark-24 Aerial Mine. On 15 May 1943, the first six planes departed for Argentia, Newfoundland with the remainder of the squadron arriving on 1 June. It was the beginning of operations for the first PB4Y-1 squadron to serve in the European Theater. In the months to come, of the original 16 crews that was formed at Camp Kearney, approximately 52 percent of the pilots and 48 percent of the crews would be killed in action or in operational accidents. The squadron's losses would only be surpassed by VB-110.

VB-103: Operations from Newfoundland
In 1941, Argentia was a small isolated fishing village, located on the rocky coast of Newfoundland, 85 miles west of St. Johns, and separated from the mainland by Placentia Bay. In January of that year, it gained international attention when Winston Churchill and Franklin D. Roosevelt met just offshore to discuss the Atlantic Charter, which was signed in August 1941. In January 1941, under the American Bases Act, the British Government granted the United

VB-105's B-8 "H" *Sea Hag* prior to take off. This photograph clearly shows the massive 110-foot long Davis Wing (Courtesy of the Dunkeswell Memorial Museum).

States a 99-year lease to build a naval base at Argentia. For the United States, Argentia would provide a year round deep-sea port, free of ice, for patrolling the North Atlantic shipping lanes. Construction began in February 1941 and by 7 December 1941, the base became operational. By 1945, over 8,000 American and Canadian military personnel would call it home.[9]

Upon arriving at their new base, VB-103 personnel found comfortable living conditions with excellent food, living quarters, and recreational facilities such as a gymnasium, movie theaters, and officer and enlisted clubs. The remoteness of Argentia required available off-duty activities on the base, as St. John's was the nearest town of any substance that could offer Liberty for military personnel. Therefore, special Liberty trips had to be planned well in advance. Otherwise, the only other pursuits were trout and salmon fishing or beer picnics.

Flight operations were conducted from Bristol Field, named in Honor of Vice Admiral Arthur L. Bristol, Commanding officer of Task Force 24 who died of Pneumonia aboard his flagship U.S.S. *Prairie* off Argentia on 20 April 1942. Bristol Field cost 9 million U.S. Dollars to build and consisted of three 5,000-foot concrete runways; they were extended to 6,000 feet before the end of the war. However, the mile-long runways didn't relieve the anxieties of VB-103 pilots taking off and landing a PB4Y-1 as Argentia presented a serious problem because of common weather conditions experienced at the new base. At times, flight operations were cancelled or returning aircraft were diverted when the airfield had to be shut down due to heavy snow or thick fog. At times, it was necessary to divert to Greenland, Iceland, or Northern Ireland. Consequently, crews carried a toothbrush and a razor.

Long patrols, necessary to reach the mid-Atlantic, required a heavy gas load as aircraft were required to return from missions with a minimum of three hours fuel supply, due to the uncertain weather conditions. Therefore, to extend range and flying time, armor plating, some of the guns, oxygen equipment, and one of the bomb bay fuel tanks were removed from the planes, which reduced the weight from 67,000 to approximately 63,000 pounds.

Once in the air, flying conditions were extremely difficult for pilots who often encountered fog, rain, sleet, and snow. Poor visibility required the use of the APS-15 radar to search for enemy submarines but even pilots couldn't rely on the instrument all the time. On several occasions, after a radar contact was made, pilots aborted attack runs when they realized they were about to bomb an iceberg. Gene McIntyre recalled, "A lot of times when you were going in on radar you didn't know what it was."[10]

Charles P. "Muck" Muckenthaler, a survivor of Pearl Harbor, and a veteran of VP-11, remembered making a memorable low visibility run in his plane *Muck's Mauler* B-5 "E" (BurAer 32035) after his radar operator picked up a blip. While the Liberator's pilot homed in on the target, Joe Powell, an Aviation Pilot (AP) manned one of the free-swinging .50-caliber machine guns in the nose. As the PB4Y-1 closed in, Muckenthaler realized it was a Newfoundland fishing vessel and ordered his gunners to hold fire but, in the nose, Powell's headphones had fallen off and he didn't hear the order and began blasting away. Muckenthaler aborted the run but not before Powell fired a few rounds at the boat. The boat was unharmed but, from then on, Powell was nicknamed "Trigger."[11]

VB-103's prime duty of sub-hunting was limited by the time they arrived as U-boats had moved out of the routine patrol areas of

Sea Hag **starting engines with Mechanic Rex McCoy standing by with a fire extinguisher (Courtesy Rex McCoy via Dunkeswell Memorial Museum).**

Party time for VB-103 officers during the squadron's early days in England. From left to right: Lt. (jg) Ken Kemper, an unknown Navy nurse, Lt. "Whiskey" Willis, Lt. Commander Bill Von Bracht (Executive Officer), Lt. Richard "Beet Eyes" Quinlan, Lt. "Coon Dog" Myers, Lt. Macdonald, and Lt. (jg) Brownell. Von Bracht would later become the squadron's commanding officer while Brownell was later killed in action while attacking the German submarine U-508 (Courtesy of the Dunkeswell Memorial Museum).

American and Canadian aircraft. However, Lieutenant (jg) Theodore S. "Swede" Thueson in the PB4Y-1 *Impatient Virgin* B-7 "G" (BurAer 32022) conducted the squadron's only submarine attack from Argentia on 12 August 1943. Thueson, a VP-23 veteran of the Solomon Islands Campaign in the South Pacific, spotted *Oberleutant zur See* Otto Erich Bluhm's fully surfaced U-760 and, approaching from the submarine's stern, he and his crew began a 22-minute battle with the vessel. On the U-boat's deck, a couple of the crew ran towards their anti-aircraft gun and began firing as the Liberator came in for a depth charge run.

While the plane's bow and top turret gunners laid down heavy fire, Thueson pickled off three depth charges but his aim was a little off and the nearest explosion occurred 50 feet off the U-boat's starboard bow. However, the blast was close enough to wash one of the U-boat's men over the side and lift the submarine out of the water. As Thueson came around for another run, the U-boat slowly submerged beneath the waves and the run was aborted. In the U-boat, the crew inspected the damage and found the explosion had bent the forward torpedo tubes. This reduced the vessel's diving speed but the U-760 managed to evade further attacks and slowly made its way to the Spanish port of Vigo on 8 September 1943 where the crew was interned.[12]

Fun and Games
Sometimes, it was necessary to break up the monotony of flying convoy, antisubmarine patrols, or training flights and Lieutenant Charles Muckenthaler was no exception. He was a brave, tenacious, and somewhat daring individual who often flew a Liberator as if it

were a barnstorming plane. On one occasion, he decided to attempt a carrier landing with *Muck's Mauler* which, given a PB4Y-1 Liberator is over 60 feet long with a wing span of 110 feet, and weighing 60,000 pounds, probably wasn't a sound idea. While on a training exercise, Muckenthaler saw the carrier U.S.S. *Ranger* steaming into Placentia Bay conducting carrier landings. He couldn't let such a chance go by so he dropped the landing gear and flaps on the Liberator and entered the landing pattern at an altitude of 100 feet. The carrier's landing deck officer didn't wave off the massive bomber but guided him in for a landing and then gave the Liberator's pilot the order to cut the engines, indicating he didn't have a problem with Muckenthaler coming down on his ship. However, Muckenthaler decided that attempting a landing probably wasn't a very good idea and aborted the landing to the relief of his crew. That night at the Officer's Club, Commander Easton and the Carrier Task Force Commander were sitting at a table, heavily imbibing in a bottle of brandy. Easton ordered Muckenthaler over and introduced him as the pilot who interfered with the Task Force Commander's operations earlier in the day. "After a lengthy admonition, which included everything but reference to my parentage, he vomited and I became the recipient, which did not reflect the demeanor of an Officer and a Gentleman."[13]

During VB-103's three-month stay at Argentia, the squadron flew 268 missions totaling 2,003 operational hours. During this period, the squadron suffered the loss of 21 men. VB-103's first loss occurred on 24 June 1943 when Lieutenant Herbert K. Reese Jr., in the Liberator *Elmundo the Great?* (BurAer 32046) failed to return while on convoy escort, 700 miles northeast of Argentia. A message intercepted later from a U-boat operating near the convoy suggests that Lieutenant Reese and his nine-man crew were shot down. It was a sobering experience for the men of 103. Before the loss of Lieutenant Reese's crew, as Gene McIntyre remembered, then a 26-year-old enlisted crew member, "We felt invincible with that little old sub down there and you're going in with all this (The Liberator). They taught us a lesson damn quick."[14]

The squadron's second loss occurred on 7 August 1943 when Lieutenant (jg) Walter B. "Zuggi" Henry and his crew of 10 were killed when their aircraft named *Wramblin Wreck* (BurAer 32037) spun into Placentia Bay while on harbor patrol. Small pieces of wreckage and only the body of Winford F. McVey (AMM3c) were recovered but the reason for the crash was never determined. VB-103 had lost 21 men while based at Argentia; it was only the beginning as the squadron prepared to leave for England.

Although operations at Argentia didn't produce any U-boat kills, the men of VB-103 were now veterans of Navy patrol operations in the North Atlantic and were about to depart for new hunting grounds, in doing so, it would become a legend in the history of American Naval Aviation. However, earning such a reputation has a price. The crews of five U-boats would forever be entombed in their steel coffins and more than three dozen men of VB-103 would also pay the ultimate sacrifice.

2

FAW-7 Squadrons to England

I'm not saying we single-handedly won the war. But we changed things. We definitely changed things.
-Gene McIntyre on the role of FAW-7 Liberators.

On 8 July 1943, The *Madcats* of VP-63, equipped with PBY-5A Catalina's with MAD (Magnetic Anomaly Detection) Gear, became the first FAW-7 squadron to operate from the United Kingdom after Admiral King sent secret dispatch 082220 to Royal E. Ingersoll, Commander in Chief, Atlantic Fleet. The dispatch directed the squadron to report to Commander, U.S. Naval Forces in Europe, for temporary assignment with British Coastal Command for Bay of Biscay antisubmarine operations (the temporary assignment of FAW-7 squadrons was to terminate on 1 November 1943 but it was later postponed indefinitely). Equipped with MAD Gear, the Catalina was viewed as a highly desirable tool to combat the U-boat menace. However, Coastal Command and the U.S. Navy soon realized the PBY, with a top speed of 90 knots, was no match for German fighters nor did the MAD gear live up to British Coastal Command's expectations.

There were two primary reasons for sending FAW-7 units to England. First, because the Germans had adopted countermeasures against Allied patrol aircraft, the number of losses among aircraft and men were rising and this required additional reinforcements. Secondly, increasing the number of patrol aircraft would result in additional U-boat kills by broadening the area of operations. Consequently, a wider search area would force U-boats to travel greater distances submerged and they would have to surface to recharge batteries thus exposing themselves to patrol aircraft. To tighten the noose around U-boats, additional American Army Air Force and Navy squadrons were requested by the British. Furthermore, as the Navy was going to take over ASW, the movement of VP-63 to the United Kingdom was the first step in building up U.S. Naval antisubmarine aviation in England, the Mediterranean, and the South Atlantic.

VP-63 under the command of Lt. Commander E.O. Wagner reported for duty with 15 PBY-5 aircraft at Pembroke Dock, Wales on 23 July 1943 and, by the end of the month, began antisubmarine

operations over the Bay of Biscay. The transfer of additional FAW-7 units to England intensified during the second week of August 1943 when Captain William H. Hamilton (later promoted to Commodore), Commander FAW-7, issued Operational Order 2-43 on 13 July 1943. Hamilton's order ended the Wing's ASW efforts from Argentia and directed several Wing squadrons to deploy to the British Isles. In short, the entire Argentia Air Group, except for Coast Guard Squadron VP-6, would began deploying to the United Kingdom.

Meanwhile in England, Air Marshall, Sir John Slessor, Commander-in-Chief of Coastal Command, issued secret dispatch

Relative Location
FAW-7 Operations
1943-1945

North Sea

St. Davids

London

Exeter   Dunkeswell

St. Eval   Plymouth

Lands End

English Channel

France

122120 that directed the movement of Army and Navy antisubmarine squadrons to bases in Britain. The fresh Army Air Force 4th and 19th Antisubmarine Squadrons (479th Antisubmarine Group) were directed to the R.A.F. base at Dunkeswell in Devon, England while the first U.S. Navy squadron, VB-103, would base at St. Eval in Cornwall. The 479th would remain with Coastal Command until the Navy Liberator squadrons were up to operational strength.[15]

German Operations

U-boats operating in the Atlantic were nearly all based in French ports on the Bay of Biscay. The Royal Air Force and Army Air Force B-24 Squadrons, with assistance from naval surface units, had been attacking U-boats on passage through the Bay of Biscay to and from their bases. It was an aggressive operation with a considerable number of U-boats being sunk and it impaired the effectiveness of those who did manage to evade the gauntlet by forcing them to make a large part of their passage through the Bay of Biscay submerged. Consequently, U-boat crews began experiencing lower morale and general aggressiveness knowing that a growing number of their brethren were falling victims to Allied aircraft. Coastal Command wanted to keep it that way.

U-boat crews called the Bay of Biscay the "valley of death" with 65 German submarines being lost in the body of water that

The United States Army Air Force (U.S.A.A.F.) began ASW operations from Dunkeswell during summer 1943. This is Lt. Frank Perdue and crew of the 19th Antisubmarine Squadron, 479th Antisubmarine Group, beside the B-24D *Biscay Belle* (Courtesy of Dunkeswell Memorial Museum).

lies between Western France and Northern Spain. Frequent, violent, storms in the bay made surface and air operations difficult to conduct and a number of whale species inhabiting the area were often confused with submarines. Moreover, military personnel unfortunate to find themselves swimming in the Bay after surviving the loss of their ship or aircraft were faced with surviving in the frigid water long enough for a rescue ship or plane to arrive.

However, the Germans were not sitting idly by as their submarines were being sunk. To counter Allied ASW operations in the Bay of Biscay and English Channel, the Germans adopted three major countermeasures. First, short and long-range fighters such as the twin-engine Junkers JU-88 were sent out to intercept Allied patrol aircraft. Secondly, some U-boats were equipped with additional anti-aircraft weapons. These boats called flak ships, sometimes operating in groups of three, posed a formidable opponent for patrol planes. Third, Allied warships in hunter-killer groups, which were often homed in on U-boats by patrolling aircraft, were subjected to bombing by German aircraft, some equipped with radio-guided bombs. Consequently, between mid-1943 and early 1944, the threat from German patrol and fighter aircraft forced Allied ships to reduce their operations in the English Channel and Bay of Biscay.

Logistical Problems

Sending heavy bomber squadrons consisting of 12 to 15 aircraft and several hundred men to Great Britain was one thing, equipping them posed a more difficult task. Supporting such units required logistical support and, since U.S. Navy squadrons were to be deployed in the United Kingdom only on a temporary commitment, no effort was made to allocate a separate stockpile of equipment and supplies. Therefore, Commander of FAW-7, Coastal Command, British Admiralty, and the Air Ministry, among others, held several conferences during the coming weeks and months concerning logistical support for Navy Liberator squadrons. From these confer-

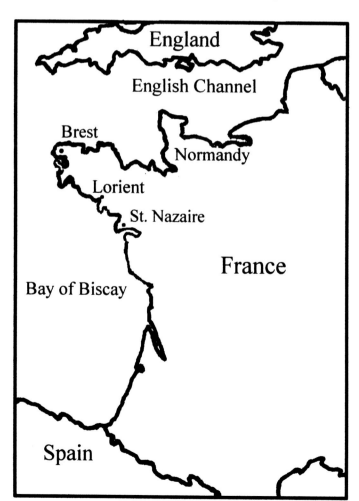

Bay of Biscay and Vicinity.

Lt. Dustin and Crew, which flew with the 4th Antisubmarine Squadron, 479th Antisubmarine Group. This aircraft continued flying with the 8th Army Air Force before returning to the US where it was broken up at Searcy Field, Oklahoma in 1945 (Courtesy of Dunkeswell Memorial Museum).

FAW-7 Headquarters building at Mount wise, Plymouth, England, with Coastal Command Headquarters No. 19 Group (Courtesy of Edward Cummings, Intelligence Officer, via Dunkeswell Memorial Museum).

ences, base facilities, equipment, armament, and aircraft spares would be obtained from the Royal Air Force and Army Air Force. However sound the plan may have seemed to the military officials concerned, it didn't meet the expectations or demands of the actual squadrons. After VB-103 arrived in England, it was obvious that relying on R.A.F. and U.S.A.A.F. logistical support couldn't meet the needs of the squadron. The major problem stemmed from the vast difference between British and American logistical support. Three logistical areas proved to be highly problematic for U.S. Navy Air Forces in Britain.

First, British Liberator squadrons themselves were operating under a severe shortage of equipment and supplies and such a shortage would obviously effect U.S.N. squadrons. Secondly, the British operated under a totally different maintenance system. While major overhaul jobs on American aircraft were performed at their own bases, the R.A.F. lacked adequate maintenance facilities for major overhauls and either used American facilities or contracted such work out to civilian contractors. There was also a shortage of R.A.F. maintenance personnel, which in the weeks to come reduced the number of operational aircraft for Navy Liberator squadron resulting in a higher number of hours flown by each aircraft per month. Finally, the British standards of housing, messing, and sanitation failed to meet Navy standards. Navy aircrews, accustomed to American constructed facilities in the United States and Newfoundland with such things as warm quarters, hot showers, and American style food, were rudely awakened when they arrived at their new accommodations in Britain.

Another view of the FAW-7 Headquarters building at Plymouth, England (Courtesy of Edward Cummings, Intelligence Officer, via Dunkeswell Memorial Museum).

The Hedron-7 Administration and Personnel Building at Dunkeswell (Courtesy of Dunkeswell Memorial Museum).

While American and British military officials ironed out the problems of supporting U.S. Naval Air Forces, Captain Hamilton on 23 August 1943, sent Secret Dispatch 211756 to Vice Admiral Patrick N.Bellinger, Commander Air Force, Atlantic Fleet, issuing FAW-7 European Theater Detachment Operation Plan No. 1-43. This established the Dunkeswell Air Group consisting of PB4Y-1 Liberator Bombing Squadrons 103 and later VB-105, and the St. Davids Group, consisting of Bombing Squadrons VB-110 and VB-111. The mission of the squadrons would be, "to prosecute the offensive by conducting and supporting Bay of Biscay operations under the operational control of British authorities. Cooperate with British Isle forces in the protection of British Isles against enemy action or infiltration. Conduct maximum possible training in all phases of air operations commensurate with missions assigned. Maintain all aircraft at highest possible state of efficiency and readiness."[16]

British Operational Control of FAW-7
The decision was made to establish FAW-7 Headquarters at the Area Combined Headquarters in Plymouth, England where the headquarters of the Royal Navy Commander-in-Chief and the Commanding Officer of No.19 Group of Coastal Command were located. The Royal Navy Commander in Chief had command of the Royal Navy Forces operating in the Bay of Biscay, western part of the English Channel, and Southwest approaches to the British Isles. The Commander of No. 19 Group had command of the Coastal Command planes operating from bases in Southwest Britain with patrol areas in the Bay of Biscay, English Channel, and adjacent waters. Since the tactical decisions concerning the disposition of aircraft in the offensive against U-boats were made at Plymouth, close communication with the Wing Commander and his British counterparts could be maintained by FAW-7.

There were two primary reasons for British operational control over FAW-7 squadrons. First, the initial commitment of U.S. Navy Air Forces was but a small fraction of the total number of planes being used in the offensive and, because the British had a complicated command organization which had achieved considerable amount of success, an independent U.S. Navy command would only complicate matters. Secondly, the general rule at the time was that the nation supplying the largest forces in an area would usually supply the commanding officer in the area and all units would come under his command.

VB-103 Arrives in the UK
On 15 August 1943, Lieutenant Commander Easton began the squadron's movement across the Atlantic with 13 PB4Y-1 Liberators departing Argentia for St. Eval, England, Cornwall, via Goose Bay, Labrador, and Reykjavik, Iceland. All planes reached their

The primary nemesis of Coastal Command and FAW-7 patrol planes was the German JU-88 twin-engine fighter. This photograph and the one that follows show the destruction of a JU-88 over the Bay of Biscay (Courtesy of Dunkeswell Memorial Museum).

Machine gun fire from a British Coastal Command plane causes flames and smoke to erupt from the JU-88's engine (Courtesy of Dunkeswell Memorial Museum).

The *Mad Cats* of VP-63, flying the Consolidated PBY5A, became the first FAW-7 squadron deployed to the United Kingdom. This photograph of a PBY-5A (BurAer 48318) was taken at Port Lyauety, North Africa. While in the UK, the plane carried a large "R" where the number 18 is located (Courtesy of Dunkeswell Memorial Museum).

destination by 17 August with the exception of one, which was delayed due to radio trouble. Meanwhile, support personnel departed by ship and faced a harrowing journey across the Atlantic.

Upon arriving at St. Eval, officer and enlisted flight personnel found out that separate living quarters had been arranged. Because of possible enemy bombing attacks against the airfield, the pilots were housed some 15 miles away at the Trevelque Hotel. The pilots didn't complain much as they were provided with daily maid service. However, Lieutenant Muckenthaler pointed out one basic fact about the separate arrangements. The pilots, safely tucked away in a hotel from enemy bombing attacks, wouldn't be able to function if the 7 or 8 enlisted members of the crew being housed at the base were killed or incapacitated. Fortunately, the Germans didn't bomb St. Eval.

For the men living at St. Eval, conditions were less than adequate. "The base lacked hot water for bathing, the quarters were cold, and straw mattresses were provided for sleeping. The food usually consisted of boiled potatoes. Boiled cabbage, boiled carrots, boiled meat, and weak tea."[17]

For VB-103 and for all future PB4Y-1 squadrons, the first couple of weeks at St. Eval consisted of training aircrews for combat over the English Channel and the Bay of Biscay. Fighter affiliation took up a substantial amount of training for new squadrons as the Germans were employing a substantial number of long and short-range fighters to attack Allied patrol planes. Using Messerschmitt Me-110 (Bf-110), Me-210, Me-410, and Junkers JU-88 fighters, the Germans often operated in groups of 6 to 12 planes and seldom attacked a B-24 unless they outnumbered her by at least 6 to 1.

Since PB4Y-1 aircraft were not equipped for night operations they operated principally by day and, therefore, a substantial number of casualties were sustained from enemy fighters. The R.A.F. tried to intercept incoming enemy aircraft with their own fighters consisting of the Supermarine Spitfire, de Havilland Mosquito, or Bristol Beaufighter. They were somewhat successful but, in the months to come, several PB4Y-1 crews would be on the receiving

end of machine gun and cannon fire from German fighters. Therefore, vigorous efforts were made to conduct gunnery practice.[18]

Commander Page Knight, a 1935 graduate of Annapolis, and a future Commanding Officer of VPB-110, owed British Intelligence for the relatively light losses of PB4Y-1s attributed to German fighters compared to those suffered by Coastal Command. Commodore Hamilton and squadron commanders were fortunate to be provided with advance information about enemy flight plans through

Three men from Hedron-7 pose for a photograph during 1943-44. From right to left: Calvin Maurier (AMM2c), Jim Brand (AMM2c), and the third (right) is unknown (Courtesy of Calvin Maurier via Dunkeswell Memorial Museum).

Lone patrol of *Calvert & Coke*, an early model PB4Y. By early 1944, most Liberators with the Plexiglas nose and the free-swinging machine guns were replaced by aircraft equipped with the ERCO bow turret (Courtesy of Dunkeswell Memorial Museum).

communiqués called, *Form Greens*, which showed the types enemy planes coming out to "greet" Allied patrol aircraft and their point of origin. Still, a considerable number of Coastal Command aircraft fell victim to German fighters.[19]

VB-103 Operations Begin

While gearing up for operations, VB-103 lost Lieutenant Commander Easton when he became the Operations Officer, and later the Chief Staff Officer, of FAW-7. On 20 August 1943, Lieutenant Commander William Von Bracht assumed command and, ten days later, with training completed; the squadron began antisubmarine operations over the Bay of Biscay. Patrol areas for Coastal Command and surface unites were identified as "Musketry" and "Sea Slug" and were established on 14 June 1943. The term "Percussion" was used to identify a patrol area west of the Iberian Peninsula (Spain) from Cape Finnistere to the latitude of Lisbon, Portugal with V-"Victor," F-"Fox," and U-"Uncle," used to identify specific areas within "Percussion." In November 1943, new patrol areas called Percussion Q-"Queen, T-"Tare," and S-"Sugar," came into use. These patrols were designed to cover the Bay of Biscay and, in addition, to catch U-boats attempting passage near the northwest coast of Spain. "Q" patrols were originally intended as night patrols for Leigh Light-equipped British Wellington bombers.[20]

Patrol Plane Commanders Lieutenant Charles "Whiskey" Willis and "Muck" Muckenthaler led VB-103's first patrols over the Bay. Both men were friends, survivors of Pearl Harbor, and veterans of PBY Catalina operations in the South Pacific. Lieutenant Charles Fountain "Whiskey" Willis was perhaps to most colorful character of FAW-7. A 24-year-old native of Beaumont, Texas, he earned the coveted naval aviator wings in May 1941 and, a few months later,

B-1 "A" of VB-103 parked on a hardstand (Courtesy of Charles Muckenthaler via Dunkeswell Memorial Museum).

Inside a hanger at Dunkeswell, B-1 "A" of VB-103 has a 120-hour check (Courtesy of Dunkeswell Memorial Museum).

reported to VP-11, a PBY-5 Catalina squadron stationed at Pearl Harbor. On the morning of 7 December 1941, Willis, Muckenthaler, and two other ensigns were at their quarters near Kaneohe when the Japanese attacked. Climbing into Willis' car, they sped towards the airfield only to be strafed by a Japanese fighter. Nobody was injured and they safely arrived at the hanger only to be strafed again by another enemy plane. This time, Willis was wounded and the Duty Officer and an ensign were killed. After recovering from his injury, he qualified as a Patrol Plane Commander and along with his crew in a PBY Catalina named *Fabulous Character*, flew 250 combat missions. His experiences in the South Pacific included attacks on a Japanese cruiser and destroyer, surviving adrift in a life raft after being shot down, and rescuing a U.S. Army General and Navy Admiral. Now, serving with VB-103 and flying a PB4Y-1 appropriately named, *Fabulous Character II*, Willis teamed up with Charles Muckenthaler and became the first PB4Y-1 Patrol Plane Commanders to fly missions over the Bay of Biscay.[21]

First Losses

Willis and Muckenthaler's patrols were routine flights as many would be in the months to come. Flying 10 to 13 hour patrols, the aircrews often didn't see anything except for the cold waters below. But, within a matter of days, the squadron began to realize the missions from England were far different than those experienced in Argentia. Flying out of England wasn't much different, weather wise, than conditions that existed in Newfoundland with rain, sleet, snow, and fog often dictating operations. The crews were used to lousy conditions at Argentia and so it wasn't much of a shock when it didn't get any better in England. However, adverse weather conditions would account for a staggering number of personnel losses. Furthermore, the enemy also brought death to Navy Liberator crews as German aircraft began pouncing on the new and inexperienced Americans.

The squadron lost its first plane and crew when, on 2 September 1943, Lieutenant Keith W. Wickstrom and his crew of eight in plane B-4 "D" (BurAer 32033) failed to return to base after an operational patrol over the Bay of Biscay. No distress calls were received by the base from the doomed plane but it appears Wickstrom's Liberator became the first PB4Y-1 to be shot down by a Junkers JU-88 of Luftwaffe's V Gruppe/Kampfgeschwader 40 (V/KG-40) a German long-range maritime fighter unit.[22]

The Junkers JU-88 C-6 was the primary fighter used by the Luftwaffe against Allied coastal patrol aircraft between 1943 and 1944. A very lethal opponent, it wasn't a fast aircraft compared to other fighters with a top speed of 310mph, approximately 30mph faster than the Liberator's top speed. However, it was very heavily armed with offensive armament consisting of three 7.92mm MG-

An inside view of a VB-110 Liberator flight deck during late 1943 or early 1944. The pilot and co-pilot are unknown (Courtesy of the Admiral James Reedy family via Gene McIntyre).

17 machineguns, one 20mm MG-FFM or MG 151/20 cannon in the nose, and two additional 20mm cannons housed in a gondola under the main fuselage. Defensive armament consisted of two rear-facing 7.92 machine guns located in the rear canopy and another 7.92 machine gun facing the rear of the gondola. In the weeks and months to come, Navy Liberator squadrons would become well acquainted with this adversary. Indeed, only two days after Wickstrom's loss, six JU-88s, of the 13/KG40 intercepted VB-103's Lieutenant (jg) James H. Alexander's bomber off the Spanish coast.

Alexander was another veteran of VP-11, who was a personable and highly respected Patrol Plane Commander. A skilful pilot, he saved the lives of eleven men on board his plane after a mission on 2 September 1943 went terribly wrong. It had been a routine patrol as the Liberator flew at 7,000 feet, heading south for the Spanish Coast. Approximately 60 miles from the coast, JU-88's were spotted flying an easterly coast at 10 to 11,000 feet, and they came down for an attack on Alexander's plane. The PB4Y-1's pilot called for battle stations as the fighters went in and began delivering a deadly hail of machinegun and cannon fire, which wounded the navigator Donald Barnett and badly damaged the bomber. While Alexander fought to evade his attackers, the Liberator's gunners

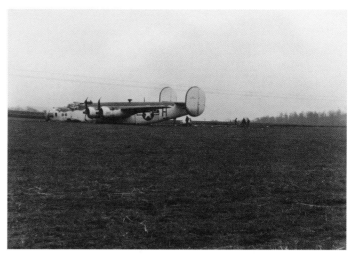

Side profile of Liberator B-8 "H" of VB-103 after returning from a patrol on 13 December 1943, it ran out of gas a few miles short of the base. The crew suffered no serious injuries (Courtesy of Gene McIntyre).

shot down *Leutnant* Gerhard Blankenberg's JU-88 fighter and damaged two others before the aerial duel ended.[23]

With his instruments shot out and three engines on fire, Alexander had no other alternative but to ditch and save as many men as possible. The Liberator, known to break apart upon hitting the water, didn't give much of a chance for all eleven men to survive the impact. Yet, there wasn't anything else Anderson could do. Through his skill, he managed to put the bomber down on the water and, by the grace of God; the entire crew exited the sinking plane and boarded a life raft.

After floating in the water for 36 hours, Alexander and his crew were picked up by a Spanish fishing vessel and taken ashore. Spain was a neutral country and the Liberator's crew spent a month recuperating before being repatriated to England. Alexander's skill earned him the Navy Cross and Purple Heart while his co-pilot, Lieutenant (jg) Paul B. Kinney and navigator Ensign Donald L. Barnett received the Distinguished Flying Cross and Purple Heart. The rest of the crew earned the Air Medal. Two months later, Alexander would be killed while participating in a training flight.

Lieutenant Commander Francis E. Nuessle and VB-105

The Navy's presence in England doubled on 5 September 1943 as the first two Liberators of VB-105 arrived at St. Eval, and by the 18th of the month, the entire squadron completed the deployment, and training began. Led by Lieutenant Commander Francis E. Nuessle, VB-105 began operational life as VP-31, a PBY-5 Catalina squadron, which served in the Caribbean, Quonset Point, and

Left: B-2 "P" VB-105 *The Solid Character*
The plane captain of *The Solid Character*, Karl Bertram, was a jazz pianist from Cincinnati and a "cool dude." The aircraft was named on his honor and Donald McDonald painted a "zoot suited jive" character on the side of the plane. The thought process is from the swing and jitterbug slang of the late 30s and early 40s. Note the 50 mission markings and one aerial kill painted below the cockpit (Information from Donald McDonald. Photograph courtesy of Dunkeswell Memorial Museum).

Parts of B-8's bomb bay doors (left) and two props lie on the ground after the Liberator came to rest on 13 December 1943 (courtesy of Dunkeswell Memorial Museum).

Props of a VB-110 Liberator turning over the English Countryside (Courtesy of the Admiral James Reedy family via Gene McIntyre).

Argentia between December 1941 and March 1943. In April 1943, the squadron was re-designated as VB-105 and traded in the PBY for the PB4Y-1.

Commander Nuessle was a combat hardened veteran and he was no stranger to the danger of of lurking U-boats. Before being promoted to Commander and leading VB-105, Lieutenant Nuessle was the commanding officer of the U.S.S. *Gannet*, a small seaplane tender. On 2 June 1942, the *Gannett* with the British ship H.M.S. *Sumarr* departed Bermuda to search for the torpedoed merchant ship *Westmoreland*. The search proved unsuccessful and the ships were ordered back to base on the afternoon of the 6th. However, during the night, the two ships became separated and, during the predawn hours of the 7th, German torpedoes hit the *Gannett* and she went down within five minutes, taking fourteen of her crew with her. Lieutenant Nuessle fought free of the ship's suction and joined some 60 survivors on life rafts, he ordered them lashed to-

gether, and the wounded brought aboard. Later that day, they were rescued. Five months later, on 1 November 1942, Nuessle became commanding officer of VP-31, the predecessor of VB-105.

After a couple of months familiarizing themselves with the Liberator, the men of VB-105 transferred to Kindley Field, Bermuda in June 1943 and began conducting antisubmarine operations. Bermuda offered the squadron a lifestyle unfamiliar to that of VB-103. While VB-103 faced inclement weather and the remoteness of Argentia Newfoundland, the men of VB-105 were forced into being subjected to such harsh living conditions and pursuits as golf, tennis, sailing, swimming, and fishing. Yet, the jaunt in Bermuda terminated in late August 1943 and the squadron left for Norfolk to be re-equipped before heading over to England.

The trip over for VB-105 aircrews proved to be uneventful and after arriving in England the aircrews began training. The tanned faces and bodies of VB-105's men quickly faded away in England's

Front profile of Liberator B-8 "H" (Courtesy of Gene McIntyre).

Lt. Commander Donald Gay, Executive Officer and later Commanding Officer of VB-110 (Courtesy of the Dunkeswell Memorial Museum).

climate and flying conditions soon reduced the number of original crews that had arrived from Bermuda. It wasn't long after arriving that Commander Nuessle lost a plane and her crew. On 10 September 1943, while on a training flight, a PB4Y-1 (BurAer 63925) piloted by Lieutenant (jg) George W. Brown, crashed into the sea off Cornwall, killing him and the crew of seven.

While, Commander Nuessle's boys trained for combat, Commander Von Bracht's squadron continued looking, unsuccessfully, for U-boats in the Bay of Biscay. However, VB-103 aircraft did encounter German fighters, which were sent out to protect submarines trying to breakout into the Atlantic from bases in France. On two separate encounters on the 16th and 18th of September, Lieutenants George Kemper and William Krausse nearly joined the list of squadron losses when their aircraft were jumped by JU-88s while on patrol. Lieutenant (jg) Kemper and his crew met up with five of the German fighters but managed to elude the attackers with minor damage to the PB4Y-1. For Lieutenant (jg) Krausse, eight JU-88s tried to bring his Liberator down during a fifteen-minute battle but his gunners managed to damage three of the pursuers.

Between Kemper's and Krausse's near brushes with death, the squadron began using the AN/CRT-1 acoustic sonobouy in an attempt to detect submerged U-boats. On 17 September 1943, Lieutenant (jg) Gail C. Burkey and his Crew Number 5, in Liberator K-103 became the first to successful use the device in European Operations. After spotting a periscope above the surface, and too late to conduct an attack after the U-boat submerged, Burkey ordered the sonobouys launched by throwing them out of the waist hatch. However, an accurate positioning of the target wasn't achieved as the aircraft wasn't carrying enough of the tracking devices and the submarine got away.

Another view of *Calvert & Coke*, which was lost on 12 November 1943 while attacking the U-508 (Courtesy of the Dunkeswell Memorial Museum).

Crew on top of the plane B-13 *Umbriago II* of VB-105. Left to right: William Reese (AMM2c), Bruce Pfeiffer (AOM2c), Lt. Donald Kinder (co-pilot), Williams (ARM2c), Lawrence Willet (AMM2c), Ensign, navigator (with crew until August 1944), Art Pivirotto (AOM2c), Jesse Riddle, Ted Werner (ARM 2c), and Lt. Whitmore (pilot) (Courtesy of the Dunkeswell Memorial Museum).

Below: *Bozo* B-5 "E" of VB-103 (BurAer 32039) in the process of being stripped of all usable parts after she crashed while landing at St. Eval in September 1943. Bottom: Here is another view of *Bozo*. Visible behind the co-pilot's station is where one of the propellers sliced through the fuselage nearly decapitating Lt. Muckenthaler (Courtesy of the Dunkeswell Memorial Museum).

Tally Ho! The Fox! There She Runs! "K" B-10 (BurAer 32015) belonged to VB-103 (Courtesy of Dunkeswell Memorial Museum).

Maintenance Problems

Being able to keep FAW-7 aircraft in the air, while depending upon the R.A.F. and A.A.F. for parts during the first months of deployment, became a major headache for the servicing unit called HEDRON-7. George Elbert, then a 19-year-old sailor attached to HEDRON, became well aware of such problems while servicing VB-103 Liberators during the fall of 1943.

"I was in charge of a very small crew who were primarily responsible for parking, fueling and making airworthiness repairs. During the St. Eval operation we were at the mercy of the R.A.F.

for anything we needed when it came to support functions. Lieutenants Willis, Muckenthaler, and their flight crews, who I then understood came out of the Pacific Theater, where things were pretty rough, drove the R.A.F. at St. Eval crazy. Though the British Airman were not openly critical of them to their faces we, as maintenance personnel, took a lot of flak because of their "gung ho" activities. In conversation, they were referred to as those "crazy American cowboys.

On one occasion, Lieutenant Willis was scheduled for a flight and his plane was in the hangar having just completed a 60-hour

Liberator "H" of VB-103 over Spain in early 1944 (Courtesy of Gene McIntyre)

Murrel E. Tittle stands on *Berlin Express* VB-103 B-13 "N" while the plane is being refueled with B-12 "M" in the background (Courtesy of Dunkeswell Memorial Museum).

The Trevelque Hotel where the officers of FAW-7 Liberator squadrons were housed while stationed at St. Eval during autumn 1943 (Courtesy of Gene McIntyre).

check. He arrived with his crew just as I was trying to get a tractor to pull it out. When he learned that the British were in the midst of one of their tea breaks, which would last another half-hour, he became furious. He ordered that I hook up the power cart, which I did, so that he could start the engines. After starting all four engines, he taxied out of the hangar leaving it looking like a war zone. Checkstands, jacks, oil drain carts, and anything loose ended up tangled or overturned in the end of the small hangar.

On another occasion, Lieutenant Muckenthaler arrived with his crew and his plane needed fuel. Again, it was British teatime and all the R.A.F. personnel were on break. He told me to have one of my men go to the nearby motor pool, drive a gas truck over to the plan, and fuel it up. This was a real no-no, first because gas was in short supply and second, we were not permitted to drive gas

Displaying 42 mission markings and an aerial kill, this is B-10 "X" for x-ray taken at Dunkeswell between 1943-44 (Courtesy of Dunkeswell Memorial Museum).

trucks for safety reasons. Our maintenance officer really caught hell for this the following day.

On another day, we needed wing jacks to put one of the planes on jacks to check a landing gear problem. After a one-day delay, the R.A.F. said there were no jacks available. That afternoon, during another teatime break, I got a truck and took three of our men to

VB-110 Crew top row (left to right): H.C. Cropsey, L. Francisco, J.O. Buchanan, and Eckelbery. Bottom: B.L. Hansen, Joe Murray, G.P. Koshiol, C. Dombrowski, N. Marx, and J. McElroy (Courtesy of Dunkeswell Memorial Museum).

VB-110 Crew (left to right): Ofstad, Carper, Francisco, Stewart, Danz, and McBride. Note this aircraft appears to have the tri-color camouflage of sea blue, intermediate blue and white/light gray (Courtesy of Dunkeswell Memorial Museum).

a nearby hangar that we occasionally used where a British four-engine bomber, with landing gear extended had been on jacks for over a week. We carefully lowered the bomber to the ground and left it rest on its landing gear and pulled the two wing jacks over to our hangar and performed our job."[24]

By fall 1943, servicing the Navy Liberators had become a major problem for the mechanics of FAW-7 and they began drawing more supplies from U.S. Navy sources. Consequently, on 21 October 1943, the inadequacy of the logistics system forced Commodore Hamilton to send a confidential letter to Admiral King, which stated,

"It is the opinion of Commander Fleet Air Wing Seven that Naval Air Forces should invariably move into foreign theaters with full and complete logistic support including rations and housekeeping personnel corresponding to the requirements of a Naval Air Facility."

The opinion of the Commodore Hamilton and the obvious consequences of operational readiness due to the current system of support would result in the establishment of the only U.S. Naval Air Facility to operate in England during World War II. Such a change wouldn't take place until March 1944 and, in the meantime, logistical support became stretched even further when additional squadrons began arriving.

The Arrival of Commander James Reedy's VB-110

On 21 September 1943, Liberators of VB-110, commanded by Lieutenant Commander James R. Reedy began arriving at St. Eval from the U.S. and, by 15 October, his squadron had finished the movement. A considerable number of men in Reedy's squadron were pulled from Patrol Squadrons 203, 209, and 211. Reedy himself had been the Commanding Officer of VP-203. Like her sister squadrons that were currently serving in England, VB-110's Liberators were the older D-model lacking a nose turret. However, the aircraft were ferried to San Diego in August while the squadron conducted state-side training and the ERCO bow turret and ASG radar where installed.

The 34-year-old Reedy was a career Navy man who attended Baldwin-Wallace College for a year before being accepted to the Naval Academy where he graduated in 1933. However, the Great Depression forced budget cuts to military spending, including personnel cuts and Reedy, having to wait for a Naval Commission, joined the Army Air Corps. After a year, his Navy Commission was granted and Reedy attended flight training. Reedy's elevation to commanding officer of a Navy Liberator squadron wasn't his first choice for an assignment. While with VP-203, Reedy and several other squadron commanders were told their squadrons would transition to the B-24 and prepare for ASW operations. At the same time, Reedy received notice to take command of a fighter squadron already serving in the Pacific. However, these orders were cancelled and a somewhat disappointed Reedy became the commanding officer of VB-110. It was an assignment he never regretted.[25]

Crew 17 of VB-110 commanded by Lt. Brougham. Rear: P. Gordon, N. Rosenberg, N. England, and H. Mack. Middle: H. Lee, J. Shekitka, and D. Fraser. Front: Lt. (jg) L. Brougham (PPC), Lt. A. Noehren, and Lt. (jg) J. Eglan (Courtesy of Dunkeswell Memorial Museum).

Crew 2 of VB-105 at Dunkeswell during October 1943. Kneeling: Rudy Zadra, Gene Zaleski, Don McDonald, Jim Henry, Bill English, B.F. Davis, Stewart Allen, and Karl Bertram. Standing: Ensign Don Kinder, Lt. Bob Nester, Lt. John Clements, and Ensign Don Curtiss (Information from Don McDonald and photograph courtesy of Dunkeswell Memorial Museum).

3

Birth of the Dunkeswell Air Group

While Reedy's and his men were training, VB-103 moved to Dunkeswell on 24 September 1943, relieving one of the Army antisubmarine squadrons. Within two months, the transfer of PB4Y-1 squadrons to Dunkeswell completed the switch of ASW operations from the Army to the Navy.

Conditions at Dunkeswell were much to be desired. During the winter, intermittent drizzle, occasionally whipped into a solid wall of water by wind, made it almost impossible to stay dry. The continuous sea of mud at Dunkeswell gave rise to the nickname of Mudville Heights. Because of rain, sleet, snow, low ceiling, and poor visibility, a considerable number of returning flights had to be diverted to other airfields. To make matters worse for the Americans, living conditions were far inferior to that accustomed to in Argentia or St. Eval. Officers and enlisted personnel alike were crowded into damp Nissen huts with inadequate heating facilities, which made it difficult to get either dry or warm. Plumbing was early Stone Age. The water supply was always low and, therefore, baths became a treat. There was no toilet paper, although rolls with the quality of laminated wood were provided plainly stamped "Government Property." Just walking around the base left any traveler with the certainty of being bathed in a sea of mud because of the narrow roads that traversed the entire airbase. However, the food supplied by Navy cooks turned out to be better than the meager meals supplied by the Royal Air Force at St. Eval.

The living conditions soon became an area of contention between the British and Americans at Dunkeswell with some in the R.A.F. complaining that the Americans seemed to want more comfort than the R.A.F. could supply and that they were asking for too much. However, an inspection by Air Commodore Lloyd was appalled at the conditions at Dunkeswell and took note on what needed to be improved.[26]

Things began looking up for the men of Mudville Heights a few weeks after their arrival as living conditions began to improve

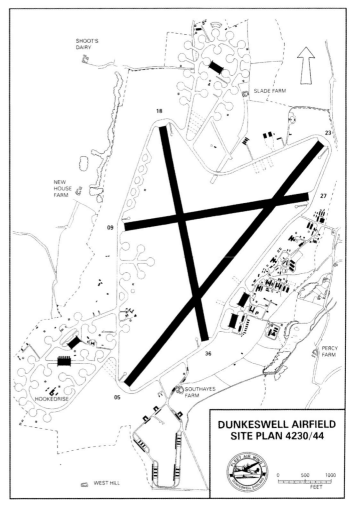

Aerial Map of Dunkeswell 1944 (Courtesy of Dunkeswell Memorial Museum).

The men who took care of the planes on the ground belonged to Hedron-7. The only man to be identified in this photograph is Carl Klenner (AMM3c) who is kneeling, third from right (Courtesy of Carl Klenner).

when oil burning stoves (the fuel was used engine oil from the planes) were installed and a Navy Construction Battalion covered the muddy roads with hard surfacing. By spring 1944, after Dunkeswell had become the only U.S. Naval Air Facility in Europe, new buildings were constructed, and luxury items, such as ice cream, became available daily at the Ship's Service Store where the men could purchase everything from cigarettes to magazines.

Removing a Dead Bird

While VB-103 began moving to Dunkeswell, the squadron nearly lost one of its most successful Patrol Plane Commanders. On 23 September 1943, Lieutenant Muckenthaler was nearly decapitated when his Liberator named *Bozo* (BurAer 32039), crashed on landing while being flown by his co-pilot, Ensign D.S. Williamson. After contacting the tower and receiving permission to land, the PB4Y-1 entered the traffic circle and made a normal approach. Before landing, Williamson received a "RED" signal from the control truck, so he pulled up and made another landing approach. The landing was made directly into the sun on a camouflaged runway, with a 30-degree crosswind of ten knots. Unknown to Williamson and Muckenthaler, the local defense unit had dug foxholes at the end of the runway. Upon landing, *Bozo* veered off the runway and Muckenthaler quickly took control of the plane and applied starboard brake and power to the outboard Number-one engine in an attempt to bring the plane back on runway. However, the plane's wheels fell into one of the foxholes, shearing off the landing gear, while the Number-three propeller sliced through the fuselage right behind Muckenthaler's headrest. Nobody was injured, but *Bozo* was demolished.[27]

When a Liberator crashed on take-off or landing, somebody had to remove it from the field and often such a task could be quite difficult if not dangerous owing to explosives that maybe on board. George Elbert remembered one unusual assignment while based at Dunkeswell when he had to clear a crashed B-24 from the end of the runway. Elbert's job, could be just as dangerous as flying missions of the Bay of Biscay

"My next assignment was removing a PB4Y which ran off the end of the runway on takeoff and came to rest in a muddy field. No sooner did we chop it up in pieces and haul it away when a second plane did the same thing. I don't recall which squadron these planes were attached to because VB-105 had already arrived, if my memory serves me correctly. I earned a rather distinctive reputation in this endeavor when it came to removing the armament in these two episodes. The British MK-24 *Zombie* was a top-secret weapon and was actually loaded and unloaded on the PB4Y's by the British. Since both crashed planes were resting on their bellies, mired in the mud, the British armament crews were not willing or able to remove the *Zombie's*, since they were considered unstable and likely to explode.

After consultation with the British, I suggested we cut the side out of the bomb bay fuselage, remove the depth charges first, which were manageable, then release the *Zombie*, allowing it to fall a short distance into the mud. We then would park our truck, which had a winch on the front end, play out all of the cable, which had a hook on the end, attach it to the *Zombie*, and then winch it to the roadway where it could be picked up and placed on a bomb truck. Needless to say, the British thought this approach was highly dangerous. In the end, this was how the problem was resolved while everyone stood their distance and watched."[28]

Change in Plans

FAW-7's presence in Great Britain continued to grow as PB4Y-1s of Commander Magruder H. Tuttle's VB-111 began arriving at St. Eval on 3 October 1943. However, the squadron's initial deployment met with disaster on 13 October when an 11-plane flight leaving Iceland for the journey to the United Kingdom encountered a violent storm over the North Atlantic. Four hours into the flight, Lieutenant "Bull" Durant's Liberator lost power to one engine and then another. On board another plane, Bill Peterson listened helplessly on his radio as Durant and his crew frantically tried to regain altitude and power. Soon, nothing else was heard from the stricken aircraft and a subseqeunt search found no wreckage or survivors.[29]

Wayne S. Zehring (AMM3c) standing next to a British Royal Navy "Seafire" that was based at Dunkeswell (Courtesy of Carl Klenner).

Because of the relatively inactivity of U-boats in the Bay of Biscay, the Commander in Chief, United States Fleet, and Chief of Naval Operations, in secret dispatches 262050 and 262052, redirected two Navy Liberator squadrons for duty in Africa to relieve two Army Liberator squadrons based in Morocco. The squadrons chosen to serve in Africa were VB-111 already based in England, and VB-112, undergoing final training in the Unites States. On 3 November, VB-111 was transferred to FAW-15 for duty in Morocco where it would stay until June 1944. Less than a year later, VB-111 would be conducting a second tour of duty in the Pacific.

By mid-October, VB-105 joined 103 at Dunkeswell and began operations over the Bay. With the movement of VB-110 later in the month, the Dunkeswell Air Group was born. On 20 October 1943, Commander William T. Easton, former commander of VB-103, took over as commander of the Dunkeswell Air Group while Commander E. O. Wagner; former commanding officer of VP-63 became commander of the St. David's Group in Wales. The St. David's Group didn't stay in existence for long as Commodore Hamilton and Coastal Command made the decision to consolidate all PB4Y assets at Dunkeswell once the 479th U.S.A.A.F. squadrons left. By the end of October 1943, VB-110 had shifted operations to Dunkeswell and, since VB-111 and 112 were being diverted to North Africa, St. David's was no longer required. Commander Wagner took control of the Dunkeswell Air Group while Commander Easton became the Air Wing's Operations Officer.[30]

Since beginning operations in August, PB4Y-1 aircrews hadn't scored a single victory against a U-boat. It wasn't due to a lack of effort. There just wasn't much U-boat activity in their area of operations. Most successes against submarines were taking place in the North Atlantic off Iceland or in the South Atlantic near the Azores. However, the Dunkeswell Air Group did claim its first confirmed attack on 24 October 1943 when Lieutenant North attacked a surfaced submarine in the Bay of Biscay. He and his crew didn't sink the submarine but the Air Officer Commanding No. 19 Group sent Lieutenant North a congratulatory note on the attack. "Lieutenant North and his crew are to be congratulated on having made an extremely well executed attack in the face of opposition from the submarine." Four months later, on 24 February 1944, Lieutenant North and his crew were shot down by German fighters and lost off the southwestern coast of England.

Four days after VB-105 arrived at Dunkeswell, the squadron began experiencing a series of interceptions by enemy fighters, which resulted in the loss of a plane and crew. One of the squadron's planes, 105-B-10, piloted by Ensign Francis F. Matthewson was attacked by six JU-88's. Luckily, he managed to take the PB4Y-1 into some cloud cover before any shots were exchanged and 105-B-10 escaped to fight another day. This encounter was the prelude to a give and take action between Coastal Command aircraft and German fighters that would continue unabated until after D-Day 1944.

Left, above: Hangar No.1 in July 1944 with the partially built Hangar No. 2. The hangars are still in use today. Left, center: A closer aerial view of the hangar area taken by a VP-63 PBY indicated by the plane's shadow in the upper right. Left, bottom: Another aerial view showing the FAW-7 Administration and Personnel Building in the upper left. (All Courtesy of Dunkeswell Memorial Museum)

The technical area where PB4Y-1s were serviced. Much of it is the same today (Courtesy of Dunkeswell Memorial Museum).

The technical area in late 1943 (Courtesy of Dunkeswell Memorial Museum).

Two days after Matthewson's narrow escape, VB-105 suffered the losses of two aircraft and crews. Lieutenant Thomas R. Evert in 105-B-2 (BurAer 63917) did not return from an antisubmarine patrol in the Bay Biscay. There were no signals received from the aircraft after takeoff but it was probably attacked by enemy aircraft and shot down. No trace of the aircraft or its crew was ever found. This loss was followed up the next day (23 October) when Lieutenant John C. Hillman in 105-B-5 (BurAer 63915) crashed on takeoff one-half mile southwest of the field killing all on board.

Maximum Effort

During November 1943, pressure from No. 19 Group forced British, Commonwealth, and FAW-7 squadrons to fly heavier schedules resulting in longer patrols. Pilots were ordered not to return to base early unless they were compelled to do so because of bad weather, enemy action, or some other emergency. Consequently, during the month, FAW-7 flew 276 operational sorties compared to 200 during October. An increase in patrols, ultimately led to additional submarine contacts, encounters with German aircraft, and

The technical area taken on 21 June 1944. A row of seven unit shops is shown in the bottom center. Note the Liberator in the bottom left with a missing wing tip (Courtesy of Dunkeswell Memorial Museum).

A Dunkeswell communal site showing the muddy conditions that existed at the base throughout the spring and winter months (Courtesy of Dunkeswell Memorial Museum).

A view of the VB-110 area showing muddy conditions (Admiral James Reedy family via Gene McIntyre)

A sign announcing the Site-4 area where VB-103 personnel were housed (Courtesy Dunkeswell Memorial Museum).

the deaths of Navy Liberator crews. VB-110 took the brunt of enemy fighter attacks and became the first squadron to lose a plane and crew during November.[31]

On 7 November, VB-110's skipper, Lieutenant Commander Reedy, evaded six JU-88s of the V/KG 40 by taking cover in the clouds. Another VB-110 crew wasn't so lucky the following day when Crew 6A, led by Lieutenant W. E. Grumbles in plane B-6 "F" (BurAer 63919) failed to return from a patrol over the Bay of Biscay. At 0937 hours, some four-and-a-half hours after Grumble's plane

took off, a plane from VB-105 intercepted a message in Morse code from B-6 "F" about being attacked by enemy aircraft. Minutes later, another transmission was heard, "SOS, SOS, SOS Potes-218..." Their doesn't seem to be any meaning to *Potes-218* and it was the last thing heard from Crew 6A of VB-110.

On the 9th, 110's Lieutenant Joseph Kennedy Jr., the older brother of a future President of the United States, nearly met a similar fate when two Messerchmitt ME-210 twin engine fighters made a run at his bomber, but Kennedy's gunners managed to drive the

Here is a living site showing that the sun did appear above Dunkeswell to dry out the roads and the men (Courtesy Dunkeswell Memorial Museum).

Personnel from VB-110 hopping aboard a truck during a rainy day at Dunkeswell (Admiral James Reedy family via Gene McIntyre)

VB-110 personnel waiting for a lift (Admiral James Reedy family via Gene McIntyre)

attackers away. Four days later, during the night of 12 November, another crew, commanded by Lieutenant J. O. Buchanan, took on eight of V/KG40's fighters in an aerial duel that lasted an hour and forty-five minutes before the PB4Y-1 found cloud cover and escaped.

Attacks on the U-966 and U-508

The Dunkeswell Air Group's job to find and attack U-boats finally paid off on 10 November 1943 when VB-105's Lieutenant Leonard E. Harmon in Liberator "R", while on antisubmarine patrol in the Bay of Biscay, sighted and attacked the surfaced U-966. Under the command of *Oberleutnant zur See* Eckehard Wolf, U-966 was spotted earlier in the morning at 0409 hours by a Wellington bomber of No. 612 Squadron. The British bomber attacked the submarine with depth charges that caused damage to the submarine's periscopes, motors, clutches, and shafts. However, after repairs were made, the

submarine was able to get under way only to be attacked by a Wellington of No. 407 Squadron, which was shot down killing the crew of six. At 0859 hours Lieutenant Harmon, the future commanding officer of VPB-105, showed up and closed in for an attack with depth charges.

Intense anti-aircraft from the U-boat greeted the Liberator causing damage to the bomb bay doors and the bomb-release circuit and Lieutenant Harmon was unable to drop. However, he pressed on the attack and continued a running battle against the enemy submarine with the PB4Y-1's gunners pouring 1,500 to 2,000 rounds of .50-caliber machine gun fire at the U-boat until a shortage of fuel forced a return to base. Three hours later, at 1145 hours, Liberator "E" of VB-103 piloted by Lieutenant (jg) Kenneth L. Wright, appeared on the scene.

Despite some anti-aircraft fire, Lieutenant Wright took the PB4Y-1 down and dropped five 325-pound depth charges with one

VB-110 personnel waiting outside their quarters at Dunkeswell in late 1943 (Admiral James Reedy family via Gene McIntyre).

Washing facilities, even primitive ones, were a necessity at the airfield where the men were often caked in mud from head to foot (Courtesy Dunkeswell Memorial Museum).

A ration line at the ship's store where personnel bought personnel items. This photograph was taken on 4 July 1944 (Courtesy Dunkeswell Memorial Museum).

The ships store with Edward W. Peckham "Physical Ed" or "push up Peckham" (right) with a cigar and fourth from the right is Edward Cunningham who was a navigator in VB-103 (Courtesy Dunkeswell Memorial Museum).

hitting close to the U-boat's port side. Coming back around after the bomb drop, the Liberator's gunners strafed the submarine, which was settling by the stern and trailing oil. At 1305 hours, VB-110 joined in the fray with Lieutenant W.W. Parish in Liberator E-110 attacking with six depth charges with one hitting the water 30 feet from the submarine's starboard side. The final attack against the U-966 occurred at 1345 hours, when a Czech Liberator of No. 311 Squadron arrived on the scene. While Lieutenant Parish faked runs on the submarine, the Czech Liberator attacked with rockets, which further damaged the vessel. Due to the damage, *Oberleutnant zur See* Wolf's submarine was unable to dive and, subsequently, he was forced to scuttle it two miles off the coast of Spain. Some of the crew survived and swam to shore or were picked up by Spanish fishing boats. After a full assessment was made on the attack, the British Admiralty awarded Lieutenant (jg) Wright 40 percent of the kill.[32]

Two days later, during the night of 12 November 1943, VB-103 chalked up another U-boat kill, but at a high cost. The action that took place during the evening of the 12th is still shrouded in mystery as the battle between Liberator and U-boat left no witnesses. In the end, VB-103 lost ten men while the Germans mourned the loss of 57 veteran submariners. While flying north of Cape Penas, Spain, Lieutenant (jg) Ralph B. Brownell in Liberator B-3 "C" named *Calvert & Coke* (BurAer 32032) spotted the Class IXC U-508 running on the surface and apparently made an attack. This submarine wasn't on her first patrol, but on it's sixth, and her crew were combat veterans. Commanded by *kapitänleutnant* Georg Staats, during the U-boat's previous patrols, it netted 14 ships totaling 78,000 tons and earned the skipper the Knights Cross.

Approaching the target, Lieutenant Brownell made his only call to base, "Am over enemy submarine in position..." and then the transmission ended. Perhaps at that point the bomber was under

Men buying items at the ships store in 1944 (Courtesy Dunkeswell Memorial Museum).

VB-110 Living area during the wet times (Courtesy Dunkeswell Memorial Museum).

The American Red Cross "Aero Club" in December 1943 (Courtesy Dunkeswell Memorial Museum).

FAW-7 personnel relax with a cold beer at the base pub (Courtesy Dunkeswell Memorial Museum).

anti-aircraft fire, and Brownell was committed to a run with depth charges. For whatever reason, *Calvert & Coke* and her crew didn't make it back to Dunkeswell. Lieutenants Willis and Muckenthaler were sent out the following day to try and locate Brownell's crew but the search only revealed two-oil slicks, one large and one small, 5 miles apart, in the vicinity of Brownell's last transmission. The slicks suggested the final resting-place for ten men on board a U.S. Navy Liberator and the crew of a German submarine. Both the hunter and hunted had fallen together.

After reviewing intercepted radio transmissions from the Germans, concerning U-508, the British Admiralty credited the Liberator's crew for the U-boat's destruction. Lieutenant Brownell received the Navy Cross, the service's second highest award, while

Ensign Daniel A. Schneider and CAP Kendall R. Poole, earned the Distinguished Flying Cross (DFC). The rest of the crew was awarded the Air Medal and all received the Purple Heart posthumously.

Operation Stonewall

By December 1943, weather conditions for flying were steadily getting worse and the number of sorties began to decline. Missions were scrubbed on six days and operations were scaled back with the Wing flying 30 less sorties than in November. The weather also played havoc on the planes and crews who did manage to get into the air. On 3 December 1943, B-13 "N" named the *Berlin Express* (BurAer 32014) piloted by Lieutenant Tony A. Lucas of VB-103 crashed into a high ridge while flying on instruments during a train-

B-1 "A" of VB-110 over the English coast and heading for home (Courtesy Dunkeswell Memorial Museum).

A three-plane flight of PB4Y-1 Liberators over the English country-side (Courtesy Dunkeswell Memorial Museum).

Hedron personnel repair a PB4Y's vertical stabilizer in the Dunkeswell repair shop (Courtesy Dunkeswell Memorial Museum).

Lt. Commander Francis Nuessle was the first Commanding Officer of VB-105. After the war, he went on to command the U.S.S. *Midway* (Courtesy Dunkeswell Memorial Museum).

Maintenance being performed on Pratt and Whitney R-1830-43/65 engines (Courtesy Dunkeswell Memorial Museum).

Testing spark plugs in the base engineering shop during May 1944 (Courtesy Dunkeswell Memorial Museum).

ing flight. All members of the crew were killed including Lieutenant (jg) James H. Alexander who had survived the ditching of his plane off the Spanish Coast in September.

For the men of VB-110, the 18th saw all five of the squadron's operational flights diverted to other bases due to miserable weather. Lieutenant (jg) G.H. Charno's crew 9B in plane B-2 "B" (BurAer 63934), attempted to make a controlled descent to Beaulieu R.A.F. Station while flying through heavy overcast. After 13 hours in the air and with only 15 minutes of fuel remaining on board, the crew

safely bailed out, while the plane, placed on autopilot by Charno, continued to fly on before running out of fuel and crashing near Manchester. Yet, even with the men risking life and limb to accomplish their missions, not a single contact with a U-boat was made by the Dunkeswell Air Group during this time.

The Germans continued their attempt to break up Allied air patrols with fighter attacks but no PB4Ys were brought down although one from VB-105 came close. On 20 December, Lieutenant (jg) Frank A. Welsh's aircraft was attacked by eight JU-88s while on patrol in the Bay of Biscay. Welsh and his crew succeeded in seriously damaging one of the enemy aircraft, while escaping with no damage to his aircraft or casualties to his crew.[33]

In early December, British Intelligence became aware of an attempt by German blockade-runners to leave French ports for the Far East and for similar vessels to attempt entry to the Bay of Biscay. Two of the ships, the *Pietro Osorno* (6,900 gross tons) and the *Alsterufur* (2,700 gross tons) became the focus of Coastal Command and FAW-7 Liberators. For the three FAW-7 Liberator squadrons, Christmas Eve 1943 was the start of a four-day running battle with blockade runners, destroyers, and torpedo boats. It began as a routine patrol day with two VB-103 Liberators piloted by Lieutenant (jg) Fred W. Felkel and Lieutenant Steele taking off from Dunkeswell at 1000 hours. At 1433 hours, a convoy of 10 to12 ships was sighted at a distance of six miles. Closing in to investigate, the aircraft came under intense anti-aircraft fire with shells bursting all around the planes. The convoy turned out to be the German blockade-runner *Osorno* and her escorts consisting of six destroyers (Z-23, 24, 27, 32, 37, and ZH-1) and two torpedo boats (T-22 and T-27). Lieutenant Felkel radioed back to base to report the sighting. After transmitting a contact report, both PB4Y-1s con-

Calvert & Coke **piloted by Lt. (jg) Stanton W. Waddell flying over Higher Longbeak, West of Marhamchurch, England during October 1943 (Courtesy Dunkeswell Memorial Museum).**

VB-110 Liberator "Q" undergoing maintenance (Courtesy of the Admiral James Reedy family via Gene McIntyre).

VB-110 Liberator "M" B-12 (BurAer 32282) flown by Crew 7 having an engine check by PATSU (Patrol Aircraft Service Unit). This aircraft was broken up at Dunkeswell in June 1945(Courtesy Dunkeswell Memorial Museum).

tinued to shadow the convoy, taking photographs, but staying out of range until ordered to return to base. Unable to land at Dunkeswell due to heavy fog, Lieutenant Felkel was diverted to Predannack, Wales; from start to finish; the mission took 12 hours and 36 minutes to complete. Felkel and his crew would get another chance to meet the German destroyers.[34]

During the late afternoon of the 24th, a VB-110 plane flown by Lieutenant Parish in plane B-5 "E" sighted a convoy of at least six ships while another VB-110 pilot, Lieutenant N. H. Hudd, reported two groups of ships. As night fell, Lieutenant Hudd attacked one group with depth charges but damage assessment, if any couldn't

be made. A few days later, Lieutenant Parish and his crew would be killed while returning from a bombing mission against the German ships.

The following day, Christmas 1943, Liberators "A" and "E" flown by Lieutenant Charles F. "Whiskey" Willis and Lieutenant George A. Enloe of VB-103 picked-up the same enemy forces. Both bombers went in to attack at different times while the ships sent up heavy flak in an attempt to bring down the patrol planes. As Willis brought his Liberator in for an attack, the bomb-bay doors failed to open fully, despite efforts by members of his crew to complete the operation manually, and he was force to abort the run. Lieutenant

B-14 "O" (BurAer 32288) of VB-110 preparing to take off from Dunkeswell N.A.F. She was broken up at Dunkeswell in June 1945 (Courtesy Dunkeswell Memorial Museum).

Liberator "B" B-2 of VB-110 comes to grief in late 1943 (Courtesy Dunkeswell Memorial Museum).

B-12 "A" another VB-110 Liberator in the air. Note the black de-icing boots on the vertical stabilizer that were used to prevent ice build up (Courtesy Dunkeswell Memorial Museum).

Enloe, a cool, calm, and courageous former PBY pilot, ran into similar difficulty when his bombs became hung up and they wouldn't drop. However, instead of returning to base, the planes made four strafing runs against the ships from an altitude of 800 feet.

Despite enemy flak, which caused some damage to the PB4Y-1, Enloe's gunners managed to inflict minor damage to a number of the German ships before being forced to return home as the convoy neared Bordeaux and an overwhelming number of German fighters approached. The Air Officer commanding No. 19 Group commended the tenacity of the two Navy Liberator crews with keeping steady contact with the fleet of enemy ships. "I very much appreciate the excellent work done by your aircraft during the last 48 hours especially A and E/103 Squadron for their shadowing this morning…which enabled me to have the last possible position of the enemy. The determination shown by the crews and the signal procedure carried out was of a high order. Well Done."[35]

Later in the day, a force of British planes was sent out to attack the *Osorno* and her escorts but they failed to make contact due to bad weather. The convoy managed to reach its destination at Gironde only to have the blockade-runner hit the sunken wreck of the *Sperrbrecher 21* (minesweeper 21). Consequently, extensive damage to the *Osorno* caused by the collision with the wrecked minesweeper forced her to be beached near Bordeaux. It was now the *Alsterufer's* turn to make the run.

The blockade-runner was found and attacked unsuccessfully on the 27th by a Coastal Command Sunderland piloted by Flight Lieutenant Bill Martin. The unsuccessful attack was only a brief reprieve for the ship as it came under attack in the afternoon by a rocket-firing Czech B-24 of No. 311 Squadron, which delivered the deathblow to the *Alsterufer*. As the blockade-runner slipped beneath the waves, the Germans, unaware of the *Alsterufer's* de-

mise, sent out a fleet of destroyers and torpedo boats to escort the merchantman into port. The following day (28 December) a PB4Y-1 from VB-105 piloted by Lieutenant Stuart D. Johnson, encountered the German escorts consisting of the 8th Destroyer Flotilla (Z-24, 27 32, 37, T-25, and 27) and the 4th torpedo boat flotilla (T-22, 23, 24, and 26). Reporting to base, he continued shadowing the force and homed in three British cruisers. Another VB-105 Liberator flown by Lieutenant Harmon arrived at the scene to assist in the shadowing and, while the two Liberator crews watched, the German escorts met up with the British cruisers H.M.S. *Glasgow* and *Enterprise*. In the ensuing surface action, the German destroyer Z-27 and torpedo boats T-25 and 26 were sunk while several more were damaged. Lieutenant Johnson's participation in locating the

Lt. "Whiskey" Willis' crew of VB-103. Back row: Charles Knauf, Hodge, Willis, Morgan, and Myer. The men in the front haven't been identified (Courtesy Dunkeswell Memorial Museum).

Over the sea, VB-103's B-14 "O"(Courtesy Dunkeswell Memorial Museum).

enemy convoy was commended by the No. 19 Group Commander. "Please congratulate captain and his crew on their faultless procedure during today's action. Accuracy of the original position of the reporting, shadowing, and homing procedure together made the ensuing surface action possible. Well Done."[36]

In the early afternoon of the 28th, the Dunkeswell Air Group mounted the largest striking force of the war as 15 PB4Y-1s, each carrying ten 350-pound bombs fitted with contact fuses, were sent out to attack the fleeing German warships. Six Liberators from VB-105, piloted by Lieutenant (jg) Robert G. Nester, Lieutenant Raymond L. North, Lieutenant Frederick G. Lathrop, Lieutenant

Edward K. Prewitt, Lieutenant Commander Donald Gay Jr., and Lieutenant John R. Crowgey, was the largest striking force to make contact with the enemy surface units. Through intense flak, the planes strafed and scored a near miss on one of the destroyers. For their respective parts in the day's actions, VB-105's Lieutenant Johnson received the Navy Cross, his co-pilot received the DFC, and the remainder of his crew received Air Medals. Lieutenant North, Lathrop, Prewitt, and their co-pilots received DFCs while the remainder of their respective crews received Air Medals.

Meanwhile, Lieutenant Commander Reedy of VB-110 leading his section failed to sight the ships and headed back to base. How-

Six planes of VB-110 head for an attack against German destroyers on 28 December 1943. One of the Liberators piloted by Lt. Parish, ran into foul weather on the return trip back to base and crashed, killing the entire crew (Courtesy of the Admiral James Reedy family via Gene McIntyre)

Fred W. Felkel and his Crew 1 flew with VB-103 and participated in the attack against German destroyers in December 1943. Felkel and his crew flew a 12-hour mission, which took them from England to North Africa (Courtesy of Fred W Felkel Jr., via Dunkeswell memorial Museum).

Lt. (jg) William H. Ryan (6th right in long coat) and crew with B-5 (BurAer 63926) of VB-110. This PB4Y-1 was lost in a crash on 28 December 1943, killing Lt. Parish and his crew (Courtesy of the Admiral James Reedy family via Gene McIntyre)

ever, they did manage to photograph a number of German survivors floating in the water. On the return flight, the section dispersed and began individual trips back to Dunkeswell. On his return, while coming out of a cloud, Lieutenant Commander Reedy encountered four German fighters. "We shot one down and that must have alerted them we were back there. Pretty soon, glowing pink balls came flying at me. I decided to use some discretion and get the hell out of there. All they had to do was dive, come back in a loop, and they would have been right on our tail. I didn't feel like sticking around since I was carrying a normal load of 10-11 depth charges and an acoustic mine." [37]

Only one of the VB-103 Liberators flown by Lieutenant (jg) Richard C. "Beet Eyes" Quinlan intercepted the enemy ships.

In the background coming in for a landing is a VB-110 Liberator returning to base after completing a mission over the Bay of Biscay (Courtesy Dunkeswell Memorial Museum).

Ensign Carlson of VB-105 with B-14 sometime during 1944 (Courtesy Dunkeswell Memorial Museum).

Enlisted personnel enjoying a bit of gambling in their quarters (Courtesy Dunkeswell Memorial Museum).

The Supply Depot at Dunkeswell Spring 1944(Courtesy Dunkeswell Memorial Museum).

Quinlan's old handle had been "Whiskey Dick" but his fellow officers renamed him "Beet Eyes" because the color of his eyes were normally beet red when he reported for morning muster. Sighting a group of six warships in line, he went after the second destroyer from 1,000 feet altitude, strafing and dropping a string of bombs. The bombs missed but the Liberator's machine gun fire caused some damage to the warship and a considerable amount of fear among its crew. Quinlan's aircraft suffered some damage but made it home.[38]

For their tenacity in attacking an enemy task force on the high seas, "Beet Eyes" Quinlan and his co-pilot Lieutenant (jg) Stanton W. Waddell were awarded the DFC and the remainder of the crew the Air Medal. Despite intense flak from German destroyers, the Dunkeswell Air Group didn't lose one plane or a single man to the enemy. However, one aircraft was lost that day when Lieutenant Parish's Liberator B-5 "E" (BurAer 63926) from VB-110, while returning to base in foul weather, crashed into a hill near Dartmoor enroute to Dunkeswell, killing him and his crew.

Detour to Gibraltar
The 29th of December saw the culmination of the Dunkeswell Air Group's attacks against the German convoy when two VB-103 Liberators, piloted by Ensign Phillip R. Anderson and Lieutenant (jg) Fred W. Felkel, were loaded with 500-pound bombs for the purpose of attacking stragglers from the enemy force. The mission would take Felkel and his men from England to Africa and earn the pilot the DFC.

After breakfast, Felkel and his crew went to the briefing room, received instructions for the mission, and departed Dunkeswell. Felkel recalls, "Take off time was 0855 and we were briefed on possibly seeing remaining German destroyers in the area that R.A.F. Beaufighters had failed to sink. To prepare us for possible attack, the plane was loaded with five 500-pound contact bombs, which were to be dropped at a minimum altitude of 1,800 feet. As we proceeded on our mission, we received radio messages at 1055 hours

to alter our course to search for dinghies and home in on the surface ships.

I remember seeing an oil slick in which there were many German sailors with only life vests and waving frantically. We circled briefly and reported this to base. We resumed patrol but we could not afford to risk dropping one of our dinghies, you could never tell when you may have a need for one."

At 1215 hours, Felkel received a message to attack the destroyers and, on completion of the mission, head for Gibraltar and land. His radar operator picked up the Spanish coast 45 miles dead ahead followed by two Spanish merchant ships approximately 25 miles off the coast. As the bomber flew on, another ship was picked up on radar at 1343 hours.

International Harvester CT-9 2 ton tractor crane lifting PSP (pierced steel planking) sections onto a truck at the railway sidings at Honiton, England. (Courtesy Dunkeswell Memorial Museum).

U-966 under attack on 10 November 1943. After being damaged by a Wellington bomber from No. 612 Squadron R.A.F., she was unsuccessfully attacked by Liberator "R" of VB-105. Between 1150 and 1315 hours, Liberators "E" of VB-103 and "E" of VB-110 attacked with depth charges followed by a rocket attack by a Czech Liberator from No. 311 Squadron R.A.F. She was finally scuttled off the coast of Spain (Courtesy Dunkeswell Memorial Museum).

"We had found our target at last, a German destroyer. He opened fire as we circled and I climbed into the clouds preparing for attack. Our bombs were spaced at 30-foot intervals to allow for a margin of error, knowing that we had no bombsight or even experience in dropping bombs from this altitude. We began our run from 2,400 feet, with air speed of 200 miles per hour, using radar as a guide, we broke out of the clouds at 1,800 feet and astern of the destroyer."

In the other Liberator, Anderson made a strafing run on the destroyer at 1,000 feet altitude, but intense flak from the enemy ship damaged the bomb release mechanism and prevented him from making a bombing attack.

On board Felkel's plane, he found it difficult to bomb the warship. "The destroyer started zigzagging all over the sea, making it almost impossible to line up the plane for a run. As we descended,

they were throwing every thing up at us but the kitchen sink. Flak was bursting all around us with intermittent "red tennis" balls streaking past us. Bill Kohel (William A. Kohel, AMM2c) was in the top turret and was holding down on the triggers of his twin 50's, empty shells were flying all over the cockpit, the noise was unbearable.

Ed Campbell (Edwin P. Campbell, AOM2c) the Bombardier, was doing his best to line up the target, "I was forced to zigzag to make a good run. Frankly, I didn't think we had a prayer of getting through this barrage of gunfire. I leveled out the plane at 1,800 feet, and Campbell dropped the five bombs mostly by guesswork. As we passed over, the tail gunner opened fire with his twin 50's, the waist gunners watched as we circled to assess the damage."

The first three bombs exploded 500, 400, and 300 feet from the port quarter, while the fourth and fifth hit approximately 100

The men of FAW-7 enjoy Christmas 1943 (Courtesy of Gene McIntyre).

In their quarters Lt. (jg) "Waddy" Waddell and Lt. (jg) "Duke" Corning try to capture the spirit of home on Christmas Eve 1943 (Courtesy of George Poulos via the B-24 Liberator Club).

Dancing at the American Red Cross "Aero Club" Christmas 1943 (Courtesy of Gene McIntyre).

Christmas party in 1943 for enlisted personnel (Courtesy of Gene McIntyre).

feet off the port beam; too far off the mark to create extensive damage. "The concussion from the explosions shook the plane violently, it seemed like it was coming apart. Miraculously, we received no direct bits in the fuselage. David Sigler told me later that be dug a piece of shrapnel out of his flight suit."

Before turning the PB4Y-1 towards Gibraltar, Felkel circled the destroyer to see the results of the attack. "We noticed it was smoking and had reduced speed to about 12 knots, still on a course of 220 degrees apparently making for an inlet by Cape Oertegal." Meanwhile, Ensign Anderson's plane was severely damaged and despite an attempt to reach Gibraltar, the crew was forced to bail out near Jerez, Spain.

Lieutenant Felkel headed his Liberator for Gibraltar but, as the sun was setting, a rainstorm was encountered and they were advised to head for Port Lyautey, North Africa. The PB4Y-1 had been in the air for nearly 12 hours when another crewman, Bill Kohel, tapped Felkel on the back and said "fuel dangerously low."

"It seemed like an eternity before we raised Port Lyautey. We requested a straight in approach once I sighted the runway. We all prayed that the fuel would hold out for just a few minutes more. Bill Kohel said I made one of the smoothest landings he had ever seen." Some 12 hours after leaving England, the Liberator touched down in Africa with approximately ten gallons of gas in two of the fuel tanks. The crew remained in Port Lyautey to have shrapnel holes patched, and the aircraft checked. Meanwhile, Felkel and his crew enjoyed the Florida-like weather in North Africa eating oranges, tangerines, and grapefruit.

Lieutenant (jg) Felkel and his crew departed Port Lyautey on New Year's Eve arriving at Dunkeswell on 1 January. He continued flying missions until 3 June 1944 when orders were cut sending him back to the United States aboard the H.M.S. *Queen Mary*. After additional training at Boca Chica N.A.S. at Key West, Florida, Felkel joined VPB-107 and flew seven missions out of Upottery Naval Satellite Facility. While stationed in England during the war, he flew 55 combat missions.[39]

4

The Chaos of War

A man grows to love his ship whether it is in mud or water.
-Lieutenant Commander Charles A. Hall
on leaving Dunkeswell in May 1944.

January 1944 brought adverse weather conditions that curtailed flying and, for 14 days, operations were scrubbed, resulting in only 104 sorties being flown by the Dunkeswell squadrons. Except for a change in command, when Commander Francis E. Nuessle turned over VB-105 to his Executive Officer, Lieutenant Commander Donald Gay Jr., the month became a series of bets on who could get their 60,000-pound bomber off the ground, complete a patrol, and return safely on ice-covered runways. For those planes that did manage to become airborne, operations for VB-103 were pretty routine until the night of 20 January 1944, when Lieutenant "Whiskey" Willis in *Zombie* B-1 (BurAer 32719), ran into heavy flak investigating a ship that turned out to be a not too friendly British naval vessel.

Willis and his crew were out in front escorting a 53-ship convoy in the Atlantic when, as the flight progressed, the radar operator picked up a blip on his screen in an area where friendly ships were not supposed to be operating. Charles Knauff, Chief Aviation Ordnanceman (ACOM), Willis' enlisted bombardier was at his station in the nose of the plane as the PB4Y-1 went down to investigate.

"We investigated and dropped a flare near where the blip showed up. It was timed to ignite as we reached it on our bombing run. When we returned on the bombing run at 500 feet, and at 250 knots, the flare ignited and showed a "Nazi Corvette." In reality, the ship was a not too friendly British warship and Willis, realizing the mistake, began taking evasive actions.

"Willis turned hard left to avoid flying over the vessel, yelling, "Don't drop, don't drop!" I put the bomb quadrant on "Safe," and started for the bomb bay and set the doors (the bomb bay doors) to closing. At this instant, the "German ship" opened fire with everything they had. One round neatly clipped the headphones from Sylvian W. Klaus, the waist gunner, leaving him with a slight scratch.

The bomber received a number of hits, which knocked out the Number-three engine and perforated the fuel tanks in the bomb bay, spilling hundreds of gallons of fuel. Willis was now flying a potential Roman Candle as the plane headed back to base. Out of range from the ship's gunners, the aft crewmen went forward to avoid the fumes accumulating in their section of the plane. Meanwhile, Willis ordered Knauff to the bomb bay to release the ordnance.

Arriving in the bomb bay, Knauff saw that the bomb bay doors were partially opened and he realized there wasn't enough room to drop the ordnance in a single salvo. One at a time, he released the

A VB-103 crew on 11 January 1944. Back row (left to right): George Reverri, Lt. Ben Steele (PPC), Ensign John Robinson (navigator), Ensign Muryl Cole (co-pilot), and Joe Summer. Front (left to right): Hank Livermont, Cliff Barker, Robert G. Anderson, Gage C. Johnson, Herb Layman, and Joe Oliver (Courtesy of Gene McIntyre).

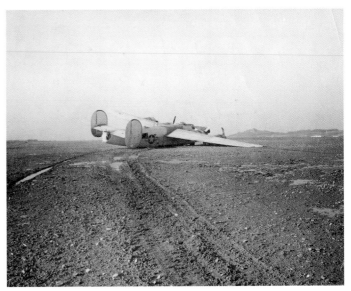

This crew from VB-110 was shot down by a JU-88 on 31 March 1944 with the loss of all hands except for two men (Lt. Chvala and Hollis) who did not make the last flight. Back row (left to right): Barton, Timberman, Ketchun, Smith, Hollis, and Chvala. Front row (left to right): Bash, Bradfield, Oliver, and Gamble (Courtesy of "Bud" Hollis via Dunkeswell Memorial Museum).

BurAer 32179 after the nose and port wheel collapsed on landing on 21 January 1944 (Courtesy via Dunkeswell Memorial Museum).

twelve general-purpose bombs and two MK-24 *Zombies*. Afterward, he went aft and threw out the two waist guns, ammunition, and anything else that wasn't nailed down to reduce weight.

"We got clearance to land in Ireland, but we believed we could make it all the way back to England, which we did. We got across Northern Ireland and landed at St. Davids, just north of Pembroke Docks. Our hydraulic system was shot up and, we had to kick the nose wheel out, crank the port side mount down, and started on the starboard mount, but it would not budge."

Without hydraulic fluid, Willis couldn't work the flaps or breaks and, therefore, as the bomber came in for a landing, he elected to

put the big bird down in the grass to minimize the possibility of creating sparks which could have ignited leaking fuel.

"It was a very smooth landing. We rolled along on two wheels for a time, and then she settled, as the wing dropped down we slowed and stopped." Willis' ability to bring back a heavily damaged bomber earned him the DFC. [40]

Attack on the U-271
The dry spell on submarine contacts ended at the end of January 1944 with VB-103 and 110 conducting two separate attacks that resulted in the sinking of one U-boat. While flying cover for con-

VB-103's Lt. Enloe in Liberator "E" attacking the U-271 on 28 January 1944 off Limerick, Ireland (Courtesy via Dunkeswell Memorial Museum).

U-271 commanded by *kapitänleutnant* **Kurt Barleben under a depth charge attack from Lt. Enloe's Liberator (Courtesy Dunkeswell Memorial Museum).**

A depth charge explodes and U-271 begins sinking by the stern (Courtesy Dunkeswell Memorial Museum).

voys SC-151 and ON-221 on the 28th, Lieutenant George A. Enloe of VB-103 in plane B-5 named, *The Bloody Miracle*, caught *Kapitänleutnant* Kurt Barleben's fully-surfaced U-271 west of Limerick, Ireland.

Before the submarine and the Navy Liberator confronted each other, Coastal Command radioed Lieutenant Enloe to provide protection for an American convoy approaching the southern coast of England. The Liberator, carrying two sonobouys, six depth charges, and a MK-24 *Zombie*, moved towards its patrol area at an altitude of 800 feet. On board *The Bloody Miracle*, Francis "Red" Dean, AOM2c, sat inside the small confines of the tail turret.

"The tail turret was a particularly cold place. When the plane is in the air and the waist hatches are open so the waist guns can be moved into firing position, the air comes in through the hatches and out through the tail turret. To make matters worse, we removed the doors from the tail turret so it is easier to get out if an emergency arose. This left the full force of the air from the waist hatches to come directly against the tail gunner's back."

Meanwhile, at his desk in the navigator's compartment, Ensign Emrick Pohling stood up, stretched, and walked over to the starboard waist hatch and, as he did, he yelled over the intercom, " I see something in the water at two o'clock, it looks like a subma-

An inspection of Dunkeswell on 13 May 1944 by Vice Admiral P.N. L. Bellinger, Commander Air Force Atlantic Fleet, with Lt. Commander James Reedy, Commanding Officer VB-110 on the left (Courtesy Dunkeswell Memorial Museum).

The commissioning ceremony on 23 March 1944 gave Dunkeswell a place in history, as it became Europe's only U.S. Naval Air Facility to operate during World War II. Left to right: Commander Francis Nuessle, Air Vice Marshal G.B.A. Baker of No. 19 Group R.A.F. Coastal Command. Commander William Easton (former Commanding Officer of VB-103), Air Vice Marshal F. H. M. Maynard, Commander G.C. Miller, Commodore William Hamilton, Commander FAW-7, and Rear Admiral G.B. Wilson, Chief of Staff to Commander US Naval Forces in Europe (Courtesy Dunkeswell Memorial Museum).

FAW-7 personnel standing at attention during the commissioning ceremony at Dunkeswell (Courtesy Dunkeswell Memorial Museum).

Rear Admiral G. B. Wilson at opening of new ship service's store (Courtesy Dunkeswell Memorial Museum).

rine." Looking out his window, Enloe confirmed Pohling's observation and began turning and putting the bomber into a steep dive. The patrol bomber closed in on the vessel and it began receiving anti-aircraft fire from the U-boat's deck gun, causing some minor damage. As the PB4Y-1 approached the target, some 500 yards away, the bombardier, Dallas Jones, ACOM (AB), opened the bomb bay doors and dropped the six depth charges as Enloe flew the plane across the U-boat at 50 feet altitude.

"Red" Dean returned fire with his turret's twin .50-caliber guns but couldn't get on target as the plane was moving too fast. "Being in the tail turret I had a full view of the submarine as we passed over it. The six depth charges straddled the sub, three landed just short of the port side; the fourth almost landed on the deck and the other two went in just over the starboard side. As the plane pulled up out of the dive the charges started going off. The number-three depth charge had gone under the sub before it exploded. They had been set for a depth of 30 feet and as they exploded, they lifted most of the sub right out of the water."

As the U-boat began sinking by the stern, Enloe turned the Liberator around and prepared to drop the MK-24 *Zombie*, however, the vessel was still above the water, and the torpedo couldn't be dropped. As the U-boat slipped beneath the waves, Enloe wanted to make sure of the submarine's destruction and ordered the sonobouys dropped. The radioman, Clifton M. LeMarr, ARM1c, reported a positive contact and the *Zombie* was launched. A few minutes later, LeMarr heard a tremendous explosion inside his headset. The Liberator circled for 30 minutes but there was no debris and Enloe headed towards the convoy. Later in the day, Enloe and his crew headed back to Dunkeswell where, after landing, the crew began their debriefing and told their story on the attack to an assembly of U.S. Navy and R.A.F. officers. As the debriefing officers were about to conclude the questioning, one of them asked if the crew had seen anything unusual about the U-boat. Dean, then nineteen years old, decided to tell them something he saw that was different about the vessel.

Ed Garloff (AMM3c) was a member of Lt. Jack Kessel's crew. He was aboard the last VB-103 plane to be lost with all hands (Courtesy of Jack Dries via Gene McIntyre).

PB4Y-1 "O" (BurAer 32023) of VB-103 taking off for a dawn patrol with Lt. Gail Burkey at the controls (Courtesy of the National Archives 80-G 282272 via Dunkeswell Memorial Museum with information from Gene McIntyre).

Crew 10 VB-105. Lt. Stevens, Lt. (jg) Taffe, Ensign Veteto, Ensign Whited W. Brooks, Charles Lindstedt, Willie Perry Williamson, R. Sweeny, G. Barry, J. Gefellnn, J. Dunn, and "Alf" Lloyd Baumann. (Courtesy of Charley Lindstedt via Dunkeswell Memorial Museum)

"I stated that there were two periscopes on the submarine's conning tower. An R.A.F. officer asked me to explain what I meant by two periscopes. I repeated there were two very distinct poles extending upward from the conning tower which looked like periscopes. With this statement, a U.S. Navy Admiral in an annoyed voice stated that German submarines only have one periscope, and since the submarine was on the surface, the periscope would not be in the raised position. I answered that this submarine did have two periscopes and they were both in the raised position. The Admiral in a loud voice said, "I repeat. German submarines do not have two periscopes you are mistaken, again." I thought to myself, with all that gold braid on the Admiral's arm, I must have been mistaken and said no more."

After the debriefing, the crew waited for the development of photographs that Roy "Slim" Carter, AMM3c, had taken during the attack while precariously hanging out the port waist hatch. Soon, the photographs were delivered and, besides showing the depth charges lifting the submarine out of the water, they showed what appeared to be two periscopes extending from the conning tower proving Dean's observation. However, he never did get an apology from the Admiral.

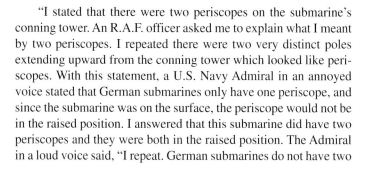

Jim Reedy hands over command of VB-110 to Lt. Commander Page Knight (with back to camera) on 28 April 1944. The other man is Lt. Commander Bob Brent, the squadron's Executive Officer (Courtesy Dunkeswell Memorial Museum).

The village of Dunkeswell and airfield's technical site as they appeared between April and May 1944 (Courtesy Dunkeswell Memorial Museum).

C. E. Gregorski and C. K. Libberton raising the Hedron-7 flag on 13 April 1944. The flag was made by Richard Keyes and Grave Evans (Courtesy Dunkeswell Memorial Museum).

Photograph taken of VB-103 personnel on 12 May 1944. Standing (left to right): Bill Kohel, Tom Henderson, Fred Felkel, Von Bracht, and Campbell. Kneeling are two men identified as Ramey and Sigler (Courtesy Dunkeswell Memorial Museum).

"The appearance of two periscope-like gear on the vessel caused a considerable amount of interest among the Navy and R.A.F. brass. For Enloe and his men, the mystery was solved a couple of days after the attack when they were invited to Coastal Command Headquarters where it was explained. They were shown enlarged photographs of the attack and explained through intelligence gathering from France. As it turned out the pipes were not periscopes but were a device known as a schnorkel, which allowed the submarine to run the diesel engines while it was submerged.

This was an important development as it reduced the time the subs were required to stay on the surface while charging their batteries. This was particularly significant to us as related to our effort to disrupt the subs progress leaving the coast of France and passing through the Bay of Biscay on their way out into the Atlantic ocean to attack our shipping. Our radar could not pick up a sub if it was submerged." [41]

Lieutenant N.H. Rudd of VB-110 in plane B-13 "N" followed Enloe's successful attack on the U-271 on the following day when he and his crew attacked a fully surfaced U-boat with depth charges while being subjected to heavy anti-aircraft fire. However, the nearest depth charge exploded some 100 feet short and the submarine apparently suffered no damage. Enloe's successful destruction of the U-271 marked the last successful attack on a U-boat by a PB4Y-1 Liberator for a considerable amount of time.

Vice Admiral Bellinger's inspection at N. A. F. Dunkeswell being introduced to Lt. Sole on 13 May 1944 (Courtesy Dunkeswell Memorial Museum).

Liberator "L" (BurAer 32169) crashed on take off at Dunkeswell on 7 May 1944 (Courtesy Dunkeswell Memorial Museum).

A flight crew unloads gear after 12-hour flight (Courtesy Dunkeswell Memorial Museum).

Surviving a Ditching

Wintry conditions persisted at Dunkeswell through February, but the number of flight operations increased over the previous month's tally. Relief for original personnel, which had begun FAW-7 PB4Y-1 operations in August 1943, finally began arriving with the issuance of a memorandum by ComAirLant on 11 February 1944. The memorandum provided for the replacement and rehabilitation of squadron flying personnel at the rate of four crews per month commencing during March. By June 1944, the pioneers of Navy Liberator operations in Europe were gone, replaced by fresh crews di-

rect from antisubmarine operations out of Port Lyautey, Africa or straight from training at Chincoteegue, Virginia. One of the replacements, Lieutenant Muryl Cole, a former PBY Patrol Plane Commander, who would complete 63 missions as a PB4Y-1 pilot with VB-103, arrived to Dunkeswell after a soggy trip from Exeter, England around 2 a.m. After a couple hours sleep he was awakened and informed to start practicing take-offs and landings for an operational mission scheduled later that day. That was his introduction to the PB4Y-1. "I'd never seen one before that." During his tour, he never received a scratch. However, the day before he was to rotate back to the United States, he was injured in an automobile accident and spent nine months at the base hospital with two broken legs.[42]

While veteran crews waited their turn for rotation, a number of Coastal Command aircraft skirmished with enemy aircraft but successfully eluded the attackers. However, on 17 February one Navy Liberator wasn't so lucky. VB-103's Crew 8 in *Worry Bird* (BurAer 32191) commanded by Lieutenant (jg) Kenneth L. Wright, while patrolling above the cloud base, was suddenly attacked by two enemy aircraft which had used cloud cover for a surprise attack.

This was Carleton F. Lillie's (AOM2c) 23rd mission. A 20-year-old bombardier and bow turret gunner, Lillie, a native of El Paso, Texas joined the Navy on 14 February 1942. Before the day was over, the crew of *Worry Bird* would join the Gold Fish Club, which acknowledges aviators that were forced to ditch their aircraft at sea. In an aerial engagement that lasted a mere three minutes, the lives of three Americans and the same number of Germans would be extinguished. For the surviving members of the crew, they would

Hedron's gift to the art world, a 8ft by 8ft mural of "Our Lady Star of the Seas" The Mural is the work of Richard McCaulay who devoted many long hours of his own time completing the work for the chapel of "Our Lady of the Seas." This photograph was taken on 21 October 1944 (Courtesy Dunkeswell Memorial Museum).

Vice Admiral Bellinger on 13 May 1944 awarding an Air Medal to Jack V. Jenkins for meritorious service performed during action against an enemy submarine. Lt. Commander Reedy is on the left of the picture (Courtesy Dunkeswell Memorial Museum).

Vice Admiral Bellinger (2nd right) Commander Air Force Atlantic Fleet, on 13 May 1944 with Commodore William H. Hamilton (3rd right), Commander FAW-7, and Commander Thomas Durfee (extreme right), Commander N.A.F. Dunkeswell (Courtesy Dunkeswell Memorial Museum).

Officers during a pre-flight briefing during Vice Admiral Bellinger's inspection to Dunkeswell on 13 May 1944 (Courtesy Dunkeswell Memorial Museum).

spend five hours in the frigid water, waiting for rescue while thinking of the possibility of their own deaths.

"Before this aerial encounter, we had been searching for a German submarine down the French coast as far south as Spain. When contact with the fighters was made, we were over the Bay of Biscay, about 50 miles off the coast of France between Brest and the English Channel."

As a bombardier, bow gunner, and trained as a navigator, the young Lillie didn't see war as a glamorous game and naturally there were times that he became outright scared. This mission was particularly troubling for Lillie because of a dream he had the night before which, in his own words was, "symbolically relevant."

"Most flyers I have known tend to be superstitious. As such, a bad dream is considered a bad omen. On the night before our mis-

Base Unit Electrical Workshop on 29 May 1944 (Courtesy Dunkeswell Memorial Museum).

Left to right are Commander Thomas Durfee, Commanding Officer NAF Dunkeswell, Vice Admiral Ben Moreell, Commander Seabees, and an unknown lieutenant (Courtesy Dunkeswell Memorial Museum).

sion, I had such a nightmare. I had a dream that l was walking down an abandoned street of an abandoned neighborhood in an unknown city. There was total absence of color except that everything appeared pallid gray.

As I walked, I was attracted to an abandoned apartment building. I entered the building and proceeded from the entry up two flights of stairs to the second floor. Before me was an open door. Beyond the door was a very large room that was devoid of all furniture except one chest-of-drawers. The top drawer had been pulled open and had been filled to overflowing with muddy water. A woman was in the process of drowning a naked newborn baby in the water.

Instead of interfering with her endeavor, I ran to report the incident to authorities. When I reached the entrance lobby, I became confused, and instead of going out the front door, I turned at the landing and continued down the stairs to the basement. Before I could stop, I found myself in the center of the basement area. I was dismayed to find I was armpit deep in water and was engulfed

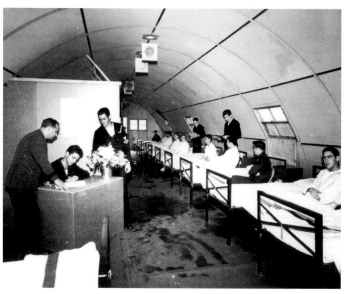

The Navy Hospital at N.A.F. Dunkeswell during May 1944 (Courtesy Dunkeswell Memorial Museum).

by snakes of all sizes."

His nightmare ended with the ringing of an alarm clock and he and his fellow enlisted crewmembers, dressed, went down to the mess hall for breakfast, and then headed for the pre-flight briefing. During the meeting, the crew was briefed on weather conditions, current operations being conducted in the Bay, and the projected path of an inbound U-boat.

For aircrews flying over the English Channel and the Bay of Biscay one aspect of reality included issuing survival kits that contained a survival map of France, chocolate bars, a compass, French Francs, and a first aid kit. For Lillie, he also carried $300 in English ten-pound notes in his pocket. As the crew headed for the plane, each man was deep in his own thoughts; Lillie's was centered on the nightmare.

"I couldn't shake the nightmare. My intuition was saying, "don't go," but the plane was nearly ready for take-off to be grounded easily (an act I had never before even considered). I was reluctant to mention the dream to Bennie Faubian, AOM2c, our tail gunner, because, in my opinion, his nervous system had crashed several weeks ago, and he was now flying on pure grit alone. I perceived the majority of the crew was too military minded to pay much heed to my concerns. The radiomen, Bob Erdman (Robert Erdman, ARM2c) and Tommy Ryan (Thomas Ryan, ARM2c), were the only two with whom I felt comfortable in sharing my dilemma. While the three of us discussed the situation, I become aware that Faubian had drifted in close enough to overhear us; so he had to be included in the conversation, Faubian immediately reminded us that we are flying *Worry Bird*. Because of its affinity for adversities, *Worry Bird* was a nickname he used to identify this particular plane.

The engines were ready to start before the four of us had developed a grounding plan. We hadn't been able to determine what equipment on the plane we could easily render sufficiently inoperable to force the flight to be cancelled. So, reluctantly, we climbed aboard, and the plane is taxied to the runway.

Bernie "The Mad Czech" Hubner (right) and Vern Ramey of VB-103. Vern Ramey is reported to have died in a drowning accident after returning to the United States (Courtesy of Jack Dries via Gene McIntyre).

Nose art of an unknown PB4Y-1 (Courtesy Dunkeswell Memorial Museum).

Crew 8 of VB-103. Top (left to right): Carlton Lillie, Robert Zabic, Kenneth Wright, Lawrence Peterson, and Robert Lacey. Bottom (left to right): Richard McDaniel, William 'Bill' Middleton, Bernie Faubian, Thomas Ryan, and Robert Erdman. Three of these men died when their plane was forced to ditch after being attacked by German fighters (Courtesy Dunkeswell Memorial Museum).

The flight started very much like all the missions before. As soon as we cleared the English coast, all guns were test fired. Everything was a "go" except for the anxiety in my stomach. This feeling was new to me, for I had never been apprehensive about previous missions. I didn't feel paranoid about this flight, but I wasn't comfortable with it either.

We flew the route the briefing officer prescribed, and checked out all the radar signals. Except for the turbulence in the weather front we recently encountered, our flight had been rather casual, and by that time, it was late in the afternoon. We headed north, back to the base at Dunkeswell."

Lieutenant Wright flew the bomber an altitude of 3,000 feet, which took him over a thick blanket of clouds. At 1634 hours, the radar operator picked up two blips on his screen, three miles distant, and announced it over the interphone. Lillie and the rest of the crew looked out and saw two silvery specks coming out of the clouds below the PB4Y-1 and heading towards their plane. They were two JU-88s climbing up fast and, as with any individual exposed to a potentially deadly situation, Lillie watched in fear thinking about what could happen to him as the fighters unleashed a hale of cannon and machinegun fire. The fighters were in line, 200 yards apart, and turning in on Wright's Liberator, the lead plane opened fire at 1,200 yards, and began scoring hits.

B-7 "U" over the airfield (Courtesy Dunkeswell Memorial Museum).

"Within a heartbeat the fighters maneuvered into position for a gunnery run and were within twelve hundred yards. There wasn't any hesitation on their part. The planes moved with precision and accuracy. At six hundred yards and within range of my 50-calibers, we exchanged fire. I saw flashes from their guns and was impressed by how slowly their tracers seemed to float toward us. (Previous to this flight, I instructed the ground crew not to include any tracers in the ammunition belts scheduled for the bow turret, for they distracted my attention from my gun sight.) For a few seconds, our bow turret, top turret and starboard waist guns trained on the Germans. Their lead plane displayed a momentary erratic wing movement, and I was reasonably sure he received damaging hits.

The air was full of tracers, and it occurred to me that for every tracer I could see there were five bullets that couldn't be seen. I heard loud impacts as their gunfire perforated our plane. One came much too close as it went through the sleeve of my electric flying suit, cut through a wool jacket, a shirt, and my long sleeved underwear. Thank God, it only burned a reddish-blue crease on the inside of my wrist without cutting the skin.

VB-103 crew of *Fearless Fosdick*. Lt. Stan Sherwin (navigator), Lt. Dave Reyner (co-pilot), Lt. Owen Windall (pilot), Don Schierenbeck (AMM3c), S. Berger (ARM3c), P.I. Derise (AMM2c), N.J. Chiarello (AOM3c), J.L. Garneau (AMM2c), R. Clark (plane Captain, AOM3c), C.W. Collier (ARM2c), N.T. Kurfiss (AMM3c) R.H. Gilbert, and dog named "Bombsite" (Courtesy Dunkeswell Memorial Museum).

Lt. George A. Enloe and Crew of VB-103's *The Kee Bird* (BurAer 32028). Rear (left to right): Lt. (jg) Kessel, Ensign Emrick Pohling, ARM1c Clifton LeMarr, AOM2c Francis Dean, and AMM3c George Carter. Front: ACOM Dallas Jones, Lt. George Enloe, AMM1c Owen Brown, AOM3c Joseph Toner, and ARM2c Ralph Allen (Courtesy Dunkeswell Memorial Museum).

Right: Muryl R. Cole at Dunkeswell 1944. He completed 53 missions with VB/VPB-103 Crew 4 and 11. He retired from the United States Navy Reserve in 1963 (Courtesy of Muryl Cole via Gene McIntyre)

Radar Technicians assigned to PATSU 7-2, Fleet Air Wing-7 outside the Radar Maintenance Shop. Photo was taken between January and May 1944. Left to right: Clyde L. McElvain (ART 2c), Ken Hallett (ART-2c), L.E. Maynard (Art2c), Harry P. Brewer (ART1c) (Courtesy of Clyde L. McElvain via Gene McIntyre).

Within those few seconds, I have been able to fire several bursts. The Germans were now at 3:30 o'clock. Relative to me, they had slid toward the tail of our plane and beyond the turning capability of my bow turret. At this point, I became a spectator. I could feel our plane vibrate as our gunners fired away and saw the flashes from the German guns. I watched tracers heading towards us and toward them from our starboard waist gun and top turret. If the Germans completed their gunnery run without breaking off, Faubian, in the tail turret, would have a chance to fire a burst or two."

During the heated exchange of gunfire, the Liberator's gunners managed to shoot down one of the attackers flown by 23-year-old *Oberleutnant* Kurt Necesany of the I/ZG who was killed along with two other crewmen. The downing of Lieutenant Wright's PB4Y-1 became Necesany's six and final aerial victory.[43]

"The fighters one and only run was over. My mouth was dry; I looked at my hands and they were steady. I put one hand on top of my head and was surprised that I was able to feel my pulse there. I decided to align my turret with the plane because I had a disturbing thought. I would be able to exit the ERCO ball turret only if I could closely align it with both the horizontal and vertical axes of the plane. As I started the maneuver, I discovered that the vertical control had apparently been shot out, but the turret had horizontal movement, So, I completed the horizontal alignment, and was excited to realize that fate arranged for the turret to be in vertical alignment before it was disabled. I would be able to get out of this trap.

During this brief encounter, my eyes had been on the fighters, but for a fleeting second, my mind drifted from reality back to a thought that had been previously interrupted. I imagined those fellows were about my age-20 years. I bet we all would have been friends if we had been raised in the same neighborhood. Except for a radioman at each of our airfields, no one in the world knew this dual took place. I wondered what in the ever-loving, blue-eyed hell this crazy war is really about.

Lieutenant Wright found concealment in the clouds that ended an aerial battle, which lasted only 30 seconds. However, the PB4Y-1 had taken some devastating hits. The number-four engine was hit and trailing a trail of smoke and several minutes later, the number-one engine went out. "Pilot Kenneth Wright instructed me to jettison our depth bombs. I complied and then abandoned the bow of the plane and joined those already in the waist section. They were Robert Lacey, Richard McDaniel, ARM2c, Robert Zabic, ACOM, Bennie Faubian, Robert Green, AOM3c, and Tommy Ryan."

Lieutenant Wright had difficulty keeping the plane on a steady course due to the damage, he couldn't keep it in the air much longer, and ditching it in the cold water was the only means of saving himself and his crew. Yet, ditching it brought the probability that some of the men wouldn't make it out of the sinking aircraft and would forever be entombed in her on the bottom of the Bay. The crew

Dunkeswell during spring 1944 (Courtesy Dunkeswell Memorial Museum).

American Red Cross serves coffee at N.A.F. Dunkeswell during spring 1944 (Courtesy Dunkeswell Memorial Museum).

VB-105 Crew 7 served together at Dunkeswell from May 1944 to April 1945. Back row (left to right): Lt. Ben Wisher, Lt. Harley Smith, Ensign John Chilton, N.E. Lassiter (AOM3c), and Edward Faye (ARM3c). Front row (left to right): L.A. Hogan (ARM3c), James W. Ross (AMM3c), Jack Stout (ARM3c), J.C. Klitch (AMM3c), and J.P. Chuostol (AMM1c). Note the R.A.F. style jackets the enlisted men are wearing. They had to wear such clothing, as the Germans did not consider U.S. Navy work clothes a uniform. (Courtesy of James W. Ross)

Water tower built to serve the airfield and dispersed living sites. It no longer exists (Courtesy Dunkeswell Memorial Museum).

prepared for ditching. Lillie's ditching station was on the deck, facing aft, with his back against a thin aluminum bulkhead that separated the waist section from the bomb bay.

"My hands clasped my knees, which were drawn up tight in front of my face. I had never been one to make a public display of my religious beliefs, but I do believe in an all-powerful Creator who has the ability to control my fate and the outcome of all events. At this critical moment in my life, I was earnestly engaged in prayer. I truly expected to cross the 'Great Divide' within the next few seconds, For the first time I can ever remember, I felt completely helpless."

The bomber hit the water, splitting the plane into three sections. Inside the sinking plane, Lillie knew he was going to survive.

Crew 12 of VB-105. J.P. Rosen (AMM2c), F.H. Wake (AMM3c), Lt. E.M. Cohen (PPC), Lt. (jg) J.J. Middleton (2nd pilot), Ensign B.L. Korty (navigator), G. Haddad (sp) (AMM2c), Ensign J. McGann (pilot-navigator), T.H. Pope (S1c), K.C. Perysian (AOM1c), J. O'Connor (S1c), and C.H. Pillow (ARM2c) (Courtesy Dunkeswell Memorial Museum).

"I felt the plane bump as it ticked the top of a couple of ground swells, then the big finale as the plane and ocean collided. What happened? I didn't remember experiencing the impact, yet I was surrounded by water, I was blind, and I heard fire crackling all about me."

Lillie couldn't see and wondered if something had hit him in the eyes and that a state of shock prevented him from feeling the pain. He felt his head for blood.

"I know what blood tastes like; so I touched my eyes and tasted my fingers. As my hand reached for my eyes, I felt a wool-lined leather helmet that was tight on my head and pushed down snugly over my eyes. I removed it, and immediately I could see again." At that point in time, Lillie was the happiest he had been in his young life, realizing that he hadn't been blinded.

"I surveyed my plight and quickly discerned that the crackling sound of the imaginary fire was being made by metal snapping in two as the writhing sea wrenched a helpless fuselage. I was on my knees in a rear bomb bay and would soon be totally engulfed in water. The command deck was buckled up, and the bulkhead I was leaning against was missing. As I faced aft, I saw daylight and headed that way. I complied with the training film and didn't pull the toggle on my life jacket while I was still in the plane.

"Everyone who was in the waist had abandoned ship without my having seen them go. Water was halfway up the opening on the side of the waist hatch. The big life raft that we carried aboard all flights was still neatly snapped shut. It looked like a giant wiener as it randomly floated about me. I tried to get it through the side hatch, but it was too slick to grasp. I decided to go out the starboard hatch while I still could, and then try to coax the raft through from my position outside the plane."

Once outside, he decided that it was time to inflate his life jacket only to find out that it had been shredded to pieces while

Crew 5 commanded by Lt. Brenegan (Courtesy of Gene McIntyre).

Beginning in March 1944, VB-103 began receiving fresh aircrews. The following photographs were taken between March and June 1944. Above: Crew 2 commanded by Lt. Binnebase (Courtesy of Gene McIntyre).

exiting the sinking plane. "Retrieving the raft was promptly forgotten as I saw Faubian facing a gaping break in the fuselage and wildly flaying his arms about. His boot was trapped in the break, and he couldn't prevent going down with the plane. I approached him from his back, put my arms around his chest, and propped both my feet against the plane. With all my strength, I tried to free his foot. Just then, the turbulent water caused the break to open a little, and his foot was freed.

He spun in the water and grabbed me in a bear hug. I didn't realize he was so strong, and I didn't know he couldn't swim. He was frantic and in the process of drowning both of us. As I try to free myself from his grip, I become strangled. I could hardly breathe, much less think logically. Finally, I got free of his grasp except for

his iron grip on my little finger. It got broken, but now we were separated.

The gyrations of the water moved me about 50 or 60 feet to where Richard McDaniel was drifting. His life jacket was inflated, and he held a small oxygen tank. When he saw that my life jacket was useless, he gave me the oxygen tank. Because I was nearly drowned, I tried to climb on top of the tank. It spun me over head down. When I surfaced, McDaniel slapped me with more then enough force to get my attention. He instructed me to hold the tank under my chin and stay still. A miracle wave carried the two of us back to the plane just forward of the wing. The remainder of the survivors were in two small rubber rafts that Middleton had released from the top of the plane."

Crew 6 commanded by Lt. (jg) Corning (Courtesy of Gene McIntyre).

Crew 9 commanded Lt. (jg) Stohmaier (Courtesy of Gene McIntyre).

Crew 12 commanded by Lt. Cunningham (Courtesy of Gene McIntyre).

Crew 16 commanded by Lt. (jg) VanHemert (Courtesy of Gene McIntyre).

As Lillie struggled in the water, the co-pilot, Lieutenant (jg) Lawrence Patterson and Bill Middleton struggled to get one of the rafts right side up. After turning it over they and Robert Lacy helped the others climb into the raft. "The sea was extremely rough with ground swells that appeared to be 20 feet high; so we decided not to inflate the seats. The rafts were attached to each other with a 10-foot line. Some order began to emerge from this chaos."

They counted heads and realized that Erdman and Ryan were missing. They didn't get out of the wreck and went down with the plane. The surviving eight men, wet and cold and facing the possibility of hypothermia, resigned themselves to spending the night in the rafts and waiting for rescue.

"Our big fur collars were turned up around our ears to protect against the wind. The trouble with this was the collars also made good water funnels. Occasionally a curl would form on top of a ground swell, and if we were under it when it broke, a ton of water came down on our heads. Then the relatively warm water in our leather flying suits was flushed out and replaced with cold seawater.

It was a long night. We could hear the drone of a plane above the noise of the sea. It headed toward us, and the pilot turned his landing lights on. He continued to come our way. He turned his lights off and veered out to sea. This incident caused me to engage in random thinking and wondered if the sub we were trying to locate was still in this area. Wouldn't it be great if he would surface and take us prisoners!"

Before morning, someone in our raft casually remarked that the pocket containing fishing tackle was not snapped to the raft as designed. It was upside down, the flap was open, and the fish hooks etc. were loose among us. My imagination was off and running again. After all, we are in air inflated rafts. I decided to check for the hooks. I discovered that I couldn't move my legs. They didn't

feel frozen. In fact, they had no feeling at all. I wanted to move my legs, but they refused to react to instructions. So I took the hands of my companions seated on each side and placed them on my chest. Together, we three slid our hands down my body and placed them under a knee. On signal, we all tried and were able to slightly move one of my legs. We repeated the process with my other leg and then we moved their legs.

The first signs of dawn appeared and someone discovered that Faubian had died during the night. We meditated on this fact in silence. My mind flashed back to that dream I had just before our mission began; did it really portend things to come? I contemplated the deaths of my three good and loyal friends. (This train of thought was renewed a few days later when the film of our last breakfast was developed. Eardman, Ryan, and Faubian were out of focus, but my image on the picture was sharp and clear. What, if any, importance should I have given to this fact? Did my subconscious mind have reason to make me apprehensive about going on that flight? Before long, we heard a plane, and I recovered from my daze.

As it came nearer, we recognized the plane to be a Sunderland-a British flying boat. The time was probably 7 or 8 a.m. We signaled to him, but he never saw us" Within an hour, another Sunderland flew near us on his patrol south. We signaled with stainless steel mirrors, but he just kept going." Not long afterward, a third Sunderland belonging to No. 461 Squadron spotted the men in the water and flew directly for them.

"This Sunderland circled and came over us within 30 feet of the water. His crew waved and threw us a big round life raft with canned water in its survival kit. Our spirits skyrocketed. The Sunderland continued to circle within a mile radius until a U.S. Navy PBY Catalina from VP-63, escorted by three fighters, relieved it. The Sunderland that first found us made one more pass, dipped alternate wing tips, and continued on his mission south. After one low run, the fighters moved up in altitude to about 3 or 4 thousand feet and flew a big circle around us. We concluded that they have been sent here to prevent our being picked up by the Germans or the French. The PBY came in over us low and slow with its engines making a popping and cracking sound as if each revolution would be its last."

Above him, Lillie made out two of his friends staring and waving out of the seaplane's waist blister. Lieutenant Peterson realized that "Whiskey Willis was at the controls of the PBY. Everybody in the raft knew Willis' reputation as a dare devil pilot and begin worrying that he might attempt a suicidal landing in the rough sea. Yet, common sense prevailed and Willis stayed in the air radioing back to base the location of the survivors. Soon, two PB4Y-1s arrived with four escorting fighters. One of the Liberators flew in low, not more than two feet above the waves.

"As it passed over us, I recognized George Moore leaning out from the port waist hatch and waving with both hands." Moore belonged to a fellow VB-103 crew led by Lieutenants Rief and Higgenbothem and this rescue typified the closeness of the men.

"The planes seemed to circle for hours. Who knew for how long, our watches hadn't worked since they were filled with salt water. Finally, the planes streaked away over the horizon. Within a few moments, they come back. They were flying low and come directly over us. They circled back and repeated their performance." At 1315 hours, after spending nearly 20 hours in life rafts, the survivors were rescued by a British Air-Sea Rescue Launch.

"A British rescue boat appeared and drew alongside the rafts and began pulling in the wet, injured, and tired Navy aircrew. " A big British sailor reached down, lifted me out of the raft, and carried me to the deck below. He supplied all the effort it took to change from my cold, wet flying gear to warm, dry pajamas. I couldn't stand alone, and wasn't much help to him."

Below deck, the Liberator's crew were guided to bunks and given a shot of hot rum to warm up. Lillie had to be assisted to his bunk where he passed out. When he awoke, the vessel has arrived in port. "We are taken from the boat to a British military hospital. I

reported that a vertebra in my neck felt as if it is fractured. The doctors ignored my concerns without ever taking an x-ray."

He found out 50 years later after arthritis set in that a vertebra had been fractured in the ditching. The crew was treated for severed frostbite, exposure, and abrasions. Within a couple of days, they were released from the hospital and sent back to Dunkeswell.

"Those British sailors risked their lives by going deep into no-man's-territory to rescue us. I will always appreciate them and admire their valor. I am especially appreciative of the big fellow who carried me from the raft. (I weighed 120 pounds soaking wet.) My thoughts at the time were only of getting dry and warm, but he was sensitive enough to perceive that in the future I might want a token remembrance of the event. So, after I was in dry pajamas, he picked up my wet leather flying suit and cut the section out of the sleeve that surrounded the bullet hole. He told me that some day I might want to show my children how close they came to not being here."

Wright's crew never flew together again, but some of them flew a couple of additional missions with other aircrews before rotating back to the United States. Lillie went back to the United States where he joined VPB-107, another Navy PB4Y-1 squadron. Months later, he was back in England, flying the same type of patrols. Between VB-103 and VPB-107, he flew 53 missions during the war.[44]

After the downing of Lieutenant Wright's Liberator, Dunkeswell aircraft continued to spot enemy aircraft with visual sightings on the 16, 17, 19, 23, and 25 February without being intercepted. However, occasionally, the German fighters were able to pursue their quarry and bring down one of the big, lumbering Liberators. On the 26th, VB-105's's Lieutenant Raymond L. North and his crew in plane B-4 "R" (BurAer 63929), failed to return from a routine operational flight over the Southwestern approaches to the United Kingdom. He signaled to base that enemy aircraft were attacking and later a S. O. S. signal was heard. North's crew had become the victims of two JU-88's piloted by *Feldwebel* Heinz Baldeweg and *Unteroffizier* Fritz Gilfert of the 3/ZG1. Before the Liberator plunged into the water, North's men were able to send Baldeweg's JU-88 down with them.[45]

Crew 17 commanded by Ensign Moore (Courtesy of Gene McIntyre).

Unknown VB-103 crew (Courtesy of Gene McIntyre).

It wasn't the only loss for the men of Dunkeswell to mourn that day as VB-110 lost an aircraft and crew when Lieutenant J.L. Williams in B-8 "H" (BurAer 63939) crashed into the Great Skelling Rock of Ireland. A 45-acre island, Skelling rises 650 feet out of the Atlantic Ocean and it's presumed that Williams' plane crashed into it and fell into the sea while returning from an operational mission.[46]

More Losses

Commodore Hamilton wanted to carry out a more vigorous campaign against the U-boats by sending patrol aircraft, escorted by fighters, closer to U-boat bases in France. Since mid 1943, the Germans had deployed a strategy to get their U-boats into the Atlantic by sending out long-range fighters to intercept Allied patrol aircraft, shadowing and attacking warships with long-range patrol and fighter planes with high altitude, dive bombing, or using radio-guided bombs. Consequently, surface units had to limit operations in the English Channel and Bay of Biscay.

Since operations by Allied warships were curtailed due to the threat from German aircraft, Allied patrol planes became the principal means of detecting U-boats, resulting in a significant increase in operations with Wing squadrons flying 327 operational sorties totaling 3,185 hours during March 1944 compared to 253 sorties in February. Consequently, because FAW-7 aircraft were flying closer to the U-boat bases at Brest, St. Nazaire, Lorient, La Pallice, and Bordeaux, its understandable that there was an increase in the number of missions, which resulted in aircraft being lost.

March 1944 and the coming of spring improved weather conditions, the establishment of Dunkeswell as a U.S. Naval Facility on the 23rd and the transfer of the Wing to the 12th United States Fleet, Admiral Harold R. Stark, Commanding. It also brought heavy operational losses for VB-110 and 103.

A combination of bad weather and an incorrect course setting caused the deaths of Lieutenant (jg) W. H. Ryan and his crew while returning from a routine mission on 12 March. While returning in plane B-6 "F" Ryan and his crew were returning to base in foul weather when he was given incorrect course by a R.A.F. ground controller. The last signal was an SOS at which radar picked up the aircraft flying near Cherbourg, France. A week later, on the 20th, VB-103 lost a crew when Lieutenant (jg) Jack C. Kessel's PB4Y-1 "L" (BurAer 32209) crashed at sea returning from an operational mission. The plane sent a SOS, but nothing else was heard from it. The following day, their ultimate fate was confirmed when search planes spotted an oil slick and empty life rafts close to Kessel's last known position.

The month continued to get worse for FAW-7 Liberator squadrons especially for Commander Reedy's with VB-110 losing two more aircraft and crews on the 31st. Lieutenant H. Barton's B-12 "M" (BurAer 63948) and B-11 "L" (BurAer 63940) piloted Lieutenant (jg) O. R. Moore became victims of the I/ZG 1's *Oberleutnant* Dieter Meister. Both PB4Y-1s were shot down within thirty minutes of each other with Barton's plane becoming the first victim. During the following day, search planes spotted burning wreckage and empty life rafts on the water that marked the positions where some 20 men died. A third PB4Y-1 nearly came to grief the same day when Lieutenant (jg) Bruce Higgenbothem, one of the pilots involved in the rescue effort of Lieutenant Wright and his crew, became the quarry of I/ZG 1's, *Oberleutnant* Gutermann. However, Higgenbothem and his crew managed to escape without becoming another victim of a JU-88.[47]

Unknown VB-103 crew (Courtesy of Gene McIntyre).

5

D-Day Operations

Through April and May 1944, FAW-7 and Coastal Command noticed a considerable reduction in U-boat activity. Consequently, squadrons flew a third less missions then in March. Therefore, in preparation for D-Day, intensive training began for the Dunkeswell Air Group with sonobouy training being one area heavily emphasized after an inspection in April revealed significant problems with training procedures and deployment of the weapon in the following areas:

Formal training had been given only to VB-103 personnel at Argentia and most of those men had already been transferred out of the Air Group by April 1944. Except during October 1943, no skilled follow-ups had been given to FAW-7 field engineers acquainted with sonobouys.

1   Training aids were inadequate.
2   Few official reports of sonobouy usage and techniques had been received by FAW-7.
3   FAW-7 suffered from a continual shortage of sonobouys. Use during operational missions showed a lack of skill in pattern placement and interpretation of sounds that would have been considerably improved had enough units been available for training.
4   Replacement crews arriving from the United States had received no buoy training before reporting for duty.[48]

The report did congratulate HEDRON-7 for a splendid job of keeping the sonobouys serviceable and by July 1944, aircrews received the required training in using the sonobouy as intended.

German U-boat activity in the English Channel and the Bay of Biscay had been reduced in preparation for the expected invasion of France. As the bulk of operational submarines were located at French bases from Brest to Bordeaux, they would immediately put to sea for the purpose of attacking surface vessels supporting the invasion. It was expected U-boats would concentrate their attacks on larger supply ships bringing in heavy equipment. To prevent such attacks No. 19 Group established an air barrier patrol, called Operation Cork, to protect the approaches in and around the English Channel between Lands End, Cornwall and to within 5 miles of the French coast.

Air patrols were planned so that a plane would patrol each part of the Cork every 30 minutes. A 30-minute interval was chosen because a U-boat used up, in a crash dive, approximately as much battery energy as could be charged into the batteries in 30 minutes of surface charging. Accordingly, Coastal Command's contention was that if a U-boat had to crash dive every 30 minutes, it would show no net gain from the time it had been able to charge its batteries while on the surface between dives. Therefore, such barrier patrols were expected to prevent the passage of surfaced U-boats into the areas where Allied convoys were operating in support of the invasion.

VB-110's weather beaten PB4Y-1 B-4 "D" (BurAer 63932) receiving attention on 29 May 1944 (Courtesy Dunkeswell Memorial Museum).

U.S. Navy Bombing Squadron VB-114 Squadron Designation 231 (No. 11) "J" (BurAer 32192). In the photograph are PPC Lt. Oren W. Clark (facing camera); 2nd Pilot Ensign Myer A. Minchen, to Clark's left; Navigator (non-pilot) Ensign Edward Ellwood to Minchen's left with his back partially to camera, not in picture-Lt. Larry A. Kirkland, 1st pilot. The entire crew consisted of Lt. Clark-Pilot Lt. Kirkland-Pilot Ensign Minchen Pilot/Navigator Ensign Elwood-Navigator Jock McGarry-Mechanic Jim Baird-Mechanic Don Burns-Radio Operator Cliff Hallas-Radio Operator Mort Salavitch-Radio Operator Jack Woods-Ordananceman and Harold Coffin-Ordananceman (Courtesy Dunkeswell Memorial Museum).

During this period, PB4Y-1 aircrews of the Dunkeswell Air Group went out day after day and night after night on 10 to 13-hour missions, but only a few sightings of enemy submarines were made. The daily grind of long patrols in a cold, noisy aircraft, of constant monitoring of the onboard radar, or looking down at tossing waves from the unforgiving Bay of Biscay, wore down aircrews. Lieutenant Owen D. Windall, a Patrol Plane Commandeer with VB-105, with prior service with VP-31, acknowledged an enemy just as deadly as cannon fire from a German fighter.

"The chief enemy of the patrol plane pilot is boredom. Boredom begets inattention, then indifference. Hundreds of hours are spent at sea with nothing to look at but an endless expanse of waves and sky."[49]

While flying tedious patrols and waiting for the invasion, fresh aircrews from the United States began arriving at Dunkeswell to relieve the "old hands." Veterans who accumulated the required 30 missions went home or in the case of some squadron commanding officers, were reassigned. On 28 April 1944, Lieutenant Commander Reedy left VB-110 to become Commander of Patrol Air Group 1, vacated by Commander Nuessle. Lieutenant Commander Page Knight took over for Reedy and, during the ensuing celebration of Knight's elevation to commanding officer at a local tavern, the invitees participated in chandelier swinging and damaging the décor of the establishment. However, because the owners were reimbursed for damages, nobody, including the new commanding officer of VB-110, was put on report.[50]

Aerial view of the VB-114 dispersal area. In the lower right is PB4Y-1 232 "K" of VB-114 (Courtesy Dunkeswell Memorial Museum).

VB-114 Crew 8 taken at Dunkeswell during 1944. Standing (left to right): Stokton, Looker, Randel, Hancox, O'Lingley, McNulty, and Brown: Front (left to right): Hoffman, Kussel, Austin, and unknown (Courtesy Dunkeswell Memorial Museum).

Three Radio-Radar Operators from VPB-114. From left to right: Don Burns, Crew 11, Ed Austin, Crew 8, and Ray Kussel, Crew 8 (Courtesy of Jerry Brotherson via Dunkeswell Memorial Museum)

Invasion

The Allied invasion of France on 6 June 1944 marked a decided change in Coastal Command's method of operations. In support of the invasion, FAW-7 Liberators were sent out to cork up the western entrance to the English Channel. Aircraft patrolled the area at regular 30-minute intervals and the number of sorties for the squadrons were shortly increased to seven a day. FAW-7 aircraft were assigned sectors designated as H-"How" which extended from Land's End to the northern tip of the Brest Peninsula. X-"X-Ray" extended southward from Eddystone Light off Plymouth. The Y-"Yoke" area extending from Start Point to the Channel Islands. On 18 June, K-"King was added and spanned an area from Portland and tip of Cherbourg Peninsula.[51]

Oil slicks, indicating the possible position of a U-boat, were to be investigated, but lingering over the area for an extended period of time, was disallowed in order to be on station at specified times to maintain complete coverage. Patrolling closer to the French coast

Lt. Adams and Crew 12 of VB-114 were stationed at Dunkeswell between June and December 1944. Standing (left to right): Massam, Mattis, Abrams, White, Fitze, and Baker. Kneeling: Massingill, Engler, Ciardi, Drennen, and Cronce (Courtesy Dunkeswell Memorial Museum).

A searchlight equipped VB-114 at Dunkeswell on 6 September 1944 (Courtesy Dunkeswell Memorial Museum).

Officers of VB-114 on the Control Tower at Dunkeswell. Left to Right: Harry Freeland, Don Williams, Bill Burns, G A Wimpey, Arthur Moorcraft, Rip Collins, and Jim Bagwell (Courtesy of Jerry Brotherson via Dunkeswell Memorial Museum)

Lt. (jg) Grover B. Cobb of VB-114. Taken inside a PB4Y-1 at the Navigation table (Aft.) This was taken at 3am with a flash bulb camera (Courtesy of Grover B. Cobb via Dunkeswell Memorial Museum).

exposed FAW-7 aircraft to a considerable amount of anti-aircraft fire from German shore batteries and a few aircraft received damage, but only one crewmember from VB-103 was wounded.

Enemy aircraft were sometimes sighted, but Allied fighter cover reduced the danger of attack to a minimum. On D+2 (8 June), Lieutenant Anderson of VB-103 briefly engaged a FW-200 with his gunner scoring a number of hits on the enemy aircraft but the latter's superior speed enabled it to flee across friendlier territory. During June, PB4Y-1 crews investigated 17 possible sub contacts and attacked, but some of these sightings were presumed to be rock or mines.

Since the skies around Britain and the coast of France now belonged to the Allies, operating during the day could be a suicidal endeavor by U-boat crews. Therefore, the cloak of darkness offered the best mode of operating in the English Channel and the

Bay for German submariners. To counter this tactic, a detachment of six Liberators from VB-114, especially equipped with the 80 million-candlepower Leigh Light, mounted under the aircraft's starboard wing, arrived at Dunkeswell from Gibraltar on 19 June.

The six crews, led by Commander L. H. McAlpine, were part of a squadron trained for low-altitude night missions against U-boats. They were a proud bunch of men, hand picked to carry out night operations against U-boats, and as Don Higgins, a veteran of the squadron said, "It was a squadron joke that we went on Oxygen at 500 feet…that was our actual operational altitude."

While the daytime Liberator crews of FAW-7 searched for the telltale wake of a U-boat, the men of 114 relied on their onboard radar. Higgins recounts, "We had two of them (radar). The main one was on the flight deck for use by the radar operator. The second screen was small and in the cockpit, so the pilots could see what

The VB-114 Squadron Office 1944 at Dunkeswell (Courtesy of Dunkeswell Memorial Museum).

Lt. Edward Watson and some of VB-114's Crew 5. The men are Cecil Jones, Grover Cobb, and Edward Watson (Courtesy of Grover Cobb via Dunkeswell Memorial Museum).

Plane No. 5 Crew 5 of VB-114 (Courtesy of Grover Cobb via Dunkeswell Memorial Museum).

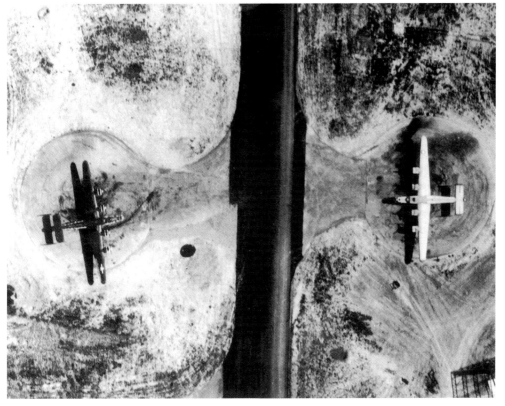

VB-110 Dispersal area. Note the variation in color schemes. On the left is BurAer 32169 of VB-114, which was the only PB4Y-1 Liberator at Dunkeswell to be painted black as an experiment. The plane was assigned to Crew 10 on a regular basis, but was also used by Crew 9 as well. This plane crashed on take off from Dunkeswell on 5 July 1944 (Courtesy of Dunkeswell Memorial Museum).

Enlisted members of VB-105 during summer 1944 (Courtesy of Dunkeswell Memorial Museum).

Inspection of the nose gear on a VB-110 Liberator. Below the ERCO bow turret is the bombardier station (Courtesy of the Admiral Reedy family via Gene McIntyre).

was happening. The radar operator on the flight deck would tell the searchlight operator when the target was one mile away and turn the light on."

The searchlight operator was located in the bow (front) of the aircraft. By looking through an astrodome, he could see forward and have a clear view of the target. When the radar operator informed him of the target, he would turn the light on to illuminate the target and keep it on during the bombing run. Because of its specialty, the squadron split up with detachments operating from Gibraltar, the Azores, and later England. While based at Gibraltar, and later the Azores, VB-114 didn't get the satisfaction of sinking

an enemy submarine. However, their contribution was keeping the submarines submerged and unable to conduct successful patrols.[52]

As the summer 1944 rolled along, FAW-7 Liberators continued to fly antisubmarine patrols and provide escorts for convoys in the English Channel, Irish Sea, and southwest approaches to England. On 18 June, Wing aircraft began flying a new patrol area called "King," which covered an area between the English coast at Portland and the tip of the Cherbourg Peninsula. This became the most easterly patrol in the "Cork" area. A month later, on 14 July, patrol "East-Easy" was established, which extended from the north of Isle Debatz off the Brest Peninsula to southwest of Ushant.

Lt. Burris and Crew 3 of VB-110 in 1944. Rear (left to right): A. Small, John Gorman, R.Watson, and C. Fowler. Center: W. Kelly, Bob Watts, G. Fowler, and G. Ridge. Front: Ensign H. Butler (navigator), Ensign J. Clark, and Lt. H. Burris (PPC) (Courtesy of Dunkeswell Memorial Museum).

Joseph S. Keeney of VB/VPB-103 next to B-12 *Piccadily Pam*, a PB4Y-1, which flew 90 missions during the course of her career at Dunkeswell (Courtesy of Jacque Morehead daughter of Joseph S. Keeney).

In early July Lieutenant Commander Von Bracht of VB-103 received orders to head home and he was relieved of command by Commander Warren Joseph Bettens. Meanwhile, on 8 July, Admiral Harold R. Stark, Commander, 12th Fleet issued secret dispatch 081724 designating FAW-7 as Task Force 121 with Commodore Hamilton as Commanding Officer.

With Allied forces in control of the sky and ground troops rapidly gaining ground in France, U-boats operations in the area were in extreme danger. On 18 August 1944, Hitler gave orders for the evacuation of the French ports of La Pallice and Bordeaux with the proviso that submarines at these ports unable to make the journey to Norway were to be scuttled. To meet this exodus, Coastal Command, and FAW-7 squadrons sent out special patrols in the Bay and English Channel to prevent U-boats from escaping. The last successful attack on a U-boat by a FAW-7 Liberator during 1944 occurred on 8 July when Lieutenant Aurelian H. Cooledge Jr., of VB-105 while patrolling off Lorient, France, joined British aircraft belonging to No. 10 Squadron on an attack against U-243.

Death of U-243

The attack on U-243 began when a Sunderland of No. 10 Squadron spotted the fully surfaced submarine, commanded by *Kapitänleutnant* Hans Martens at 1435 hours, off La Rochelle. A depth charge attack left the sub dead in the water and by 1500 hours, the sub crew began abandoning ship. At 1441 hours, Cooledge's PB4Y-1 was flying at an altitude of 800 feet when the radar operator reported a contact dead ahead at a distance of 8 miles. Three minutes later, the submarine was sighted along with a British Sunderland. Cooledge decided to attack at once and ordered battle stations as the PB4Y-1 approached from the submarine's port quarter at a speed of 200 miles per hour. Coming in at 200 feet, the puffs of the U-boat's anti-aircraft fire began to appear in front and to the sides of the approaching Liberator and a number of explosions from bursting shells rocked the aircraft.

As Cooledge's plane came within range, his top and bow turrets opened fire scoring numerous hits on the U-boat's conning tower. Cooledge pressed the bomb release button but nothing hap-

A VB-110 PB4Y-1 Liberator cruising alongside another U.S. Navy patrol plane, the PV-1 Ventura (Courtesy of the Admiral Reedy family via Gene McIntyre).

Joseph S. Keeney of VB/VPB-103 poses at the ready (Courtesy of Jacque Morehead, daughter of Joseph S. Keeney).

Lt. George Charno of VB-110 spotted German survivors from a destroyer that was sunk while trying to enter the English Channel to attack allied shipping (Courtesy of Douglas S. Peterson via Dunkeswell Memorial Museum).

pened. The pilot pulled up and into a left turn while the equipment was checked, to determine why the depth charges didn't drop. All appeared to be in working order so Cooledge took the Liberator in for a second attack. The run was made at 150 feet altitude and the bomber passed directly over the U-boat's bow. The submarine's anti-aircraft fire was noticeably weaker, but still enough to bounce the approaching plane around. Cooledge pressed the bomb release button and again the depth charges failed to release.

The check of the bombing circuits was made as the Liberator again circled the submarine and they were found to be set correctly. The Sunderland was still circling as the Liberator's crew took their gun stations once more to start a third run. When the plane was in a favorable position for starting a bow attack, Lieutenant Cooledge turned and started his attack run. Just after he did so, he sighted a second Sunderland below and ahead of him also in an attack run. The interval between the planes was sufficient for both planes to make attacks without interference so the run was continued. The explosions from the Sunderland's depth charges raised a plume of water nearly 200 feet high and obscured any view of the submarine as the blast tossed the Liberator violently upward. As the plume subsided, the submarine again became visible on the far side of the explosion area. The Liberator now descended to about 80 feet altitude and at a speed of 200 miles per hour. As the plane reached the release point, Cooledge pressed both his own release button and that of the co-pilot's and the depth charges dropped out of the bomb bay. Meanwhile, the Liberator's gunners didn't open fire on the run because there was the danger of hitting the Sunderland. The target was obscured for a few seconds by the water, but when the plume started to subside, the tail turret resumed strafing.

The bombs fell along the starboard side of the submarine approximately 25 feet from the stern and somewhat more near the bow. The co-pilot sitting in the bomb bay was able to watch the bombs fall and enter the water close alongside the U-boat. The plane now began to circle the area to await results. The depth charges

exploded and, within a few minutes of the final attack, the bow of the submarine was seen to rise vertically and then it went down stern first.

Since the PB4Y-1 had taken rather severe punishment from the flak and depth charge explosions, and because three large planes over one group of survivors from the U-boat was a little too awkward, Lieutenant Cooledge decided to move a few miles to the west to rearrange and check his equipment. During the next hour and a half contact with the survivors was lost and at 1705 hours a message was received from Dunkeswell to return to base. The return was uneventful and the plane landed at 1933 hours. Ships of the 14th Escort Group were homed by the Sunderlands to the site of the sinking and rescued 38 of the submarine's crew, including *Kapitänleutnant* Martens, who later died from his wounds.[53]

After the destruction of the U-243, the Dunkeswell Air Group settled in for nearly six months of routine patrols. By mid-July 1944, as the Allies consolidated their positions in France, the daily effort by FAW-7 was reduced to five planes per squadron per day as U-boat contacts diminished. Consequently, by 6 August, the Cork patrols were cancelled. However, some attacks against submarines were conducted during the month. On the 8th, VB-110's Lieutenant Duffy and his crew spotted a schnorkel in the English Channel. After sonobouys were launched, which indicated a positive contact and an unsuccessful depth charge attack was conducted. The Liberator's radio operator heard an underwater explosion through

A U-boat under attack by Liberator "B" VB-110 on 18 June 1944 (Courtesy of Dunkeswell Memorial Museum).

A U-boat under attack by "E" B-5 (BurAer 63952) piloted by Lt. Filson of VB-110 on 22 June 1944. A schnorkel is visible in the lower front (Courtesy of Dunkeswell Memorial Museum).

Depth charges dropped by Liberator "E" B-5 failed to sink the submarine (Courtesy of Dunkeswell Memorial Museum).

his headset but there was no visual evidence of the submarine's destruction. Two days later, another VB-110 Liberator flown by Lieutenant Seymour met with a very determined U-boat crew near Lorient, France. While attacking the surfaced submarine with depth charges and machine gun fire, the Liberator encountered heavy flak causing minor damage to the plane. Seconds before the depth charges exploded, the enemy vessel was able to submerge without any apparent damage.

The withdrawal of U-boats from French ports coincided with the end of enemy fighter interception of FAW-7 Liberators. The last encounter took place in mid-August between VB-105's Lieutenant John T. Hitchcock and a DO-217. During the brief engagement, the PB4Y-1 gunners apparently inflicted light damage to the enemy aircraft but it escaped.

During this period, when patrols were becoming more and more routine and, with the possibility that the war would be over in a matter of months, the idea of remembering the men who had paid the ultimate sacrifice while serving with FAW-7 Liberator squadrons came about. Some 400 men donated over $1,200 U.S. Dollars to enable St. Nicholas, the Anglican Church in Dunkeswell, to in-

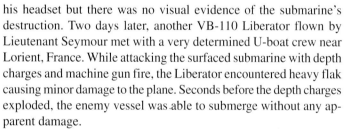

The schnorkel can still be seen during the explosions (Courtesy of Dunkeswell Memorial Museum).

T-2 Hangar No.5 under construction 8 July1944 (Courtesy of Dunkeswell Memorial Museum).

T-2 Hangar No.5 under construction (Courtesy of Dunkeswell Memorial Museum).

stall a memorial organ. The instrument is still in use today and is a tribute to the sacrifice and charity of the men who served at the Naval Air Station during the Second World War.

Joseph P. Kennedy Jr. and Special Air Unit 1

In the summer of 1944, American and British Intelligence believed that a massive steel and concrete tunnel complex at Mimoyecques, near Pas DeCalais, France was associated with the German V-weapon campaign, specifically, the V-1 and V-3 rockets. Moreover, the Germans were in the process of building the Hochdruckpumpe (High Pressure Pump), a 459-foot super cannon capable of sending a 300-pound artillery shell to London, some 90 miles away. Since August 1943, Mimoyecques and other V-weapon facilities had been repeatedly bombed by British and American air forces without any noticeable effect. However, on 6 July 1944, a British Lancaster bomber dropped a 12,000-pound "Tall Boy" bomb that damaged

T-2 Hangar No.5 under construction (Courtesy of Dunkeswell Memorial Museum).

the facility to such an extent that work on the Hochdruckpumpe was halted. However, without this knowledge, an operation was organized to take out the fortification by destroying it with a pilotless aircraft filled with over 20,000 pound of high explosives. Special Air Unit 1 was assigned the job.

Special Air Unit 1 (SAU-1) was organized at Fersfield, England on 23 July 1944, consisting of 11 officers and 16 enlisted men with one PB4Y-1 Liberator designated as the BQ-8 drone plus two PV-1 radio control aircraft with television equipment for use in guiding the drone. This gear allowed the control aircraft to direct the drone from a distance and hence to avoid the dangers posed by enemy anti-aircraft defenses. The BQ-8 required two men to get the aircraft into the air and set the controls. Once the radio controls were set, they were to simply bail out of the flying bomb as a mother ship guided the drone to the target. The target selected by the Army Air Corps for the first operation of the Special Air Unit was the fortifications at Mimoyecques. What the operation lacked were volunteers to fly the drone.

The commanding officer of SAU-1, Jimmy Smith, was a Naval Academy classmate of Commander James Reedy, former commanding officer of VB-110. Reedy was a man who wouldn't send out men for a mission that he wasn't prepared to go on himself and thus volunteered for the first special mission. However, Commodore Bill Hamilton didn't agree to the reassignment and made his objection known. "You (Reedy) will not go off on flights like that. Your business is to run the group." Consequently, Reedy needed to find somebody else to do it, and the 29-year-old Joseph Kennedy was the first to volunteer and would become the first Navy pilot to fly the BQ-8.[54]

Young Joe, earmarked for greatness by his father, perhaps even the presidency of the United States, never lived to see his full potential. He was the eldest son of Joseph and Rose Kennedy and the older brother of John who would become President of the United States and, like his older brother, he would meet a tragic death. After earning his wings in May 1942, Kennedy served with Com-

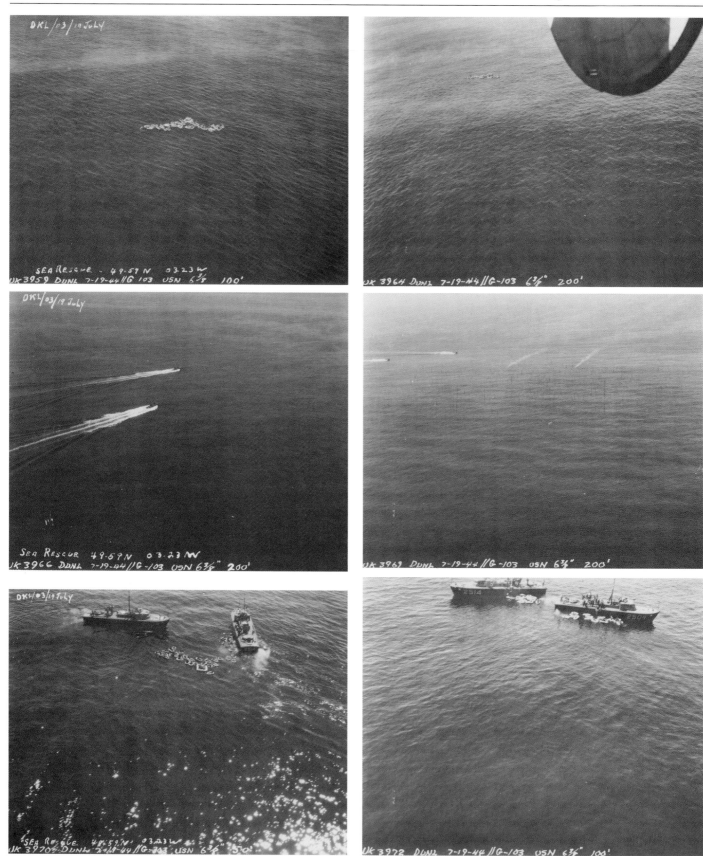

Although the primary duty of FAW-7 squadrons was to hunt down German U-boats, such units were often called on to provide convoy coverage or locating the survivors of a sunken ship or downed aircraft (Air Sea Rescue). The six photographs above show a PB4Y-1 participating in an Air Sea Rescue effort (*see individual captions on opposite page*).

Combat Air Crew Mess with Crew from VB-114 before a night patrol on 11 August 1944. Lt. Oren Clark and crew (Courtesy of Dunkeswell Memorial Museum).

mander Reedy in VP-203 and by October 1943, he was serving as a Patrol Plane Commander with VB-110. Among the squadron's commissioned officers, he was considered a fine, often roguish individual, but an exceptional naval aviator. However, some of the enlisted men that knew Kennedy had less than favorable thoughts about him. Some remember Kennedy for leaving an enlisted man out all night in subfreezing temperatures to fix the guns on his plane's tail turret or the time when he left his crew out on the tarmac during a bitterly cold day while he hitched a ride back to base.[55]

Joseph Kennedy's tour of duty as a Navy Patrol Plane Commander in England, like so many others that flew them, was long and tedious. Kennedy did the job that was asked of him. He flew

Photos Opposite, Top left: Survivors in their one-man life rafts look up as Liberator "G" of VB-103 comes on seen in the English Channel (Courtesy of Tony Sivo via Dunkeswell Memorial Museum). Top right: The Liberator passes by the survivors (background) at an altitude of 200 feet (Courtesy of Tony Sivo via Dunkeswell Memorial Museum). Center left: Two rescue boats race towards the survivors (Courtesy of Tony Sivo via Dunkeswell Memorial Museum). Center right: The rescue boats home in on two smoke flares dropped by the PB4Y-1 (Courtesy of Tony Sivo via Dunkeswell Memorial Museum). Bottom left: The rescue boats pull alongside the survivors as the Navy Liberator passes over at 50 feet (Courtesy of Tony Sivo via Dunkeswell Memorial Museum). Bottom right: The survivors are pulled aboard the vessels as the aircraft passes by at 100 feet (Courtesy of Tony Sivo via Dunkeswell Memorial Museum).

the required number of missions, spotted a possible U-boat or two, and evaded enemy fighters. Yet, when his original tour ended, Kennedy didn't leave, instead, he continued flying until the day he died. The real reason behind his fatal decision to stay in England will never be known. Was it due to patriotism or blind ambition to become a war hero? Such status during that time was an important criterion for entering American politics. Or was it because of his father's request to watch his sister who was engaged and about to be married to a Protestant Englishman? Such questions have circulated for over half a century among historians and political scientists and will, in all probability, be the topic of discussion for the next hundred years. No matter what his intentions were, he chose to participate in a dangerous undertaking and in that, Joe Kennedy cannot be faulted. In a report submitted by SAU-1 two days after the accident, his enthusiasm and that of his co-pilot was noted. "Lieutenants Kennedy and his co-pilot Wilfred J. Willy were aware of the risks but confident and enthusiastic of its success."[56]

In a secluded hanger, a war-weary Liberator named *Zootsuit-Black* (BurAer 32271), was prepared for its last flight, and guarded around the clock by Navy guards. The plane was ordered gutted and everything that wasn't required to fly the ship was removed in order to load it with over 21,000 pounds of Torpex high explosives. One of the men picked to strip the aircraft was 19-year-old Willie Newsome, an enlisted member of FAW-7 who remembered the event in the present tense as veterans often do when they tell of their experiences. He was told before entering the hanger to conduct his work in stripping the plane, "You go in there and you don't tell anybody what you see." To him, after the plane had been stripped, "it looked like a ghost ship."

The mission of 12 August 1944 called for Lieutenants Kennedy and Willy to fly the BQ-8 drone from the R.A.F. base at Fersfield and to ensure that flight control was transferred to the two accompanying PV-1 mother ships. The pilots then would parachute from the drone over English territory and afterward, the PV-1s would direct the explosive-laden aircraft to the vicinity of Mimoyecques. The mother ships could operate outside the range of the German anti-aircraft defenses while directing the drone against the target.

George Koshiol of VB-110 (foreground) with PB4Y-1 "D" B-4 in the background (Courtesy of George Koshiol via Dunkeswell Memorial Museum).

The wheel of a VB-110 Liberator hitting the runway at Dunkeswell after another long patrol (Courtesy of George Koshiol via Dunkeswell Memorial Museum).

Crew briefing VB-110. This photograph was taken illicitly and confiscated for the duration by the Commanding Officer of VB-110 (Courtesy of Dunkeswell Memorial Museum).

The BQ-8 would detonate either upon contact with the ground or by remote control from the PV-1s.

Kennedy lifted the grossly overloaded flying bomb *Zootsuit Black* off the ground at Fersfield with the intention of destroying the German weapon site. He didn't fulfill his mission. Some 21 minutes after taking off, at 6:20 PM, the aircraft exploded in midair killing Kennedy and Willy. The burning pieces of wreckage floated to the ground, covering a five-square mile area. The explosion was thorough and complete and no human remains were recovered. For sacrificing their lives, Kennedy and Willy received the Navy Cross

posthumously. After his eldest son's death, Joseph Kennedy Sr., looked upon his second son John to become President.

Kennedy's death didn't end operations for SAU-1 and a second attempt on 3 September 1944 by another member of VB-110, Lieutenant Ralph Spalding, was more successful. His drone, loaded with 24,000 pounds of Torpex, hit near a V-2 rocket site at Heligoland and proved the potential use pilotless weapons. Yet, Spalding, who earned the Navy Cross for his participation with SAU-1, would also die tragically four months later when a PB4Y-1 named, *The Green Banana* (BurAer 63944), he was ferrying back to the United States crashed in Morocco killing all on board.

Dunkeswell, August 1944. Crew 28 of VB-110. Top (left to right): Norman England, Harold Mac, John Shekitka, Donald Fraser, Howard Lee, Norman Rosenberg (Ross), and Paul Gordon. Bottom: Lt. (jg) Brougham (co-pilot), Lt. Noehren (pilot), and Lt.(jg) Egan (navigator) (Courtesy of Dunkeswell Memorial Museum).

U-243 under attack on 8 July 1944 by PB4Y-1 "T" of VB-105 and Sunderland "H" and "K" of No.10 Squadron Royal Australian Air Force (R.A.A.F.) (Courtesy of Dunkeswell Memorial Museum).

Crew 7 Top row (left to right): Lt. (jg) Carl Holt, Ellis G. Kelly (ACMM), Lt. John H. Shaffer (PPC), Ensign Fridley (navigator), and Donald E. Dirst (ARM1c). Bottom row: Earl Inman (AMM3c), Dennis F. Kelly (AMM3c), Jerry Goldberg (AOM3c), William Spillman (ARM3c), and Jack Lowry (ARM3c) (Courtesy of Dunkeswell Memorial Museum).

Joseph P. Kennedy Jr., during flight training in 1942 (Courtesy of Dunkeswell Memorial Museum).

Joseph Kennedy in late 1943 while serving with VB-110 (Courtesy of the Admiral James Reedy family via Gene McIntyre).

Joe Kennedy at the controls of a PB4Y-1 while serving with VB-110 (Courtesy of Dunkeswell Memorial Museum).

Kennedy (center) and his crew standing next to Liberator "B" B-2" (Courtesy of the Admiral James Reedy family via Gene McIntyre).

Joe with Gil Rapp at Dunkeswell relaxing in the sun (Courtesy of the Admiral James Reedy Family via Gene McIntyre).

Living quarters of Joe Kennedy at Dunkeswell (Courtesy of Dunkeswell Memorial Museum).

PB4Y-1 "K" B-10 of VB-110. In the background is a PV-1 Ventura (Courtesy of the Admiral Reedy family via Dunkeswell Memorial Museum).

Kennedy at Fersfield Airfield on the day he died (Courtesy of Dunkeswell Memorial Museum).

35-year-old Lt. Wilford J. Willy was killed along with Joseph Kennedy on 12 August 1944 (Courtesy of Dunkeswell Memorial Museum).

VB-110 flight line with Liberator "Q" in the forefront (Admiral Reedy family via Courtesy of Dunkeswell Memorial Museum).

The crew of a VB-110 Liberator in the front of plane B-12 (Courtesy of the Admiral Reedy family via Gene McIntyre).

Enlisted Men's Mess Hall on 8 July 1944 (Courtesy of Dunkeswell Memorial Museum).

Grass cutting near one of the runways at Dunkeswell during August 1944 (Courtesy of Dunkeswell Memorial Museum).

Crew 5 of VB-103 taken before leaving for England in 1944. Back row (left to right): Robert Mayer left the crew before going to England, Renfro Pace, D.C. Pinholster, unknown, unknown, R.H. Roberts, Marco Vaccher. James R. Alsop, and Joseph Kirchdorfer. Front (left to right): unknown, Lt. Dwight Nott, Plane Commander, and Ensign John S. Walker (Courtesy of Dunkeswell Memorial Museum).

Navy construction workers laying concrete during summer 1944 (Courtesy of Dunkeswell Memorial Museum).

6

The Dry Spell

As 1944 moved into August and September, the number of U-boat contacts began to diminish rapidly with Faw-7 Liberators making only two during the month. However, operations never wavered with additional patrols being sent to the northwestern approaches to Britain specifically, to the north and west of Ireland. Wing aircraft assigned to this sector operated under the control of 15 Group, R.A.F. with patrols beginning on 11 September.

Operations Compromised?

French and Spanish fishing boats were and still are a common sight in the Bay of Biscay. However, during the war, Coastal Command began to believe some of them were operating as picket boats to alert German fighters on the positions of Allied patrol planes. Since a few FAW-7 Liberators had been lost in the general vicinity of the fishing boats, the Bay was closed to all surface craft and all unidentified vessels would be deemed an enemy and attacked. Before imposing the ban, FAW-7 aircrews began dropping leaflets written in French and Spanish declaring the area as a danger zone. Gene McIntyre a member of Crew 5 of VB-103 remembers dropping the leaflets and placing a few rounds across the bows of fishing boats to get their attention.

During one such encounter on 6 August 1944, Fred Wake AMM2c, the bow gunner with VB-105's Crew 12 commanded by Lieutenant (jg) E. M. Cohen, fired on a suspicious fishing vessel

The following series of photographs show the daily life of a typical PB4Y-1 Liberator crew in England from start to finish. ARM2c E.J. Griffin, Crew 17 of VB-110 wakes at 3am for a patrol on 18 September 1944 (Courtesy of Dunkeswell Memorial Museum).

Crew 17 having breakfast before the mission (Courtesy of Dunkeswell Memorial Museum).

The men that formed Crew 17 stand by PB4Y-1 B-3 "C" (BurAer 63921). Back row: Patrol Plane Commander Lt. R.E. Greiwe (2nd from right). AMM1c E.E. Stoner, Ensign F.T. Angotti, Lt. R.E. Greiwe, Ensign J.O. Crites. Front row: AOM2c D.H. Noddin, ARM3c A.J. Tatum, S1c W. Raven, AMM1c E.R. Burfield, and AMM3c M.M. Joy (Courtesy of Dunkeswell Memorial Museum).

Crew 17 receiving instructions in the operations room before a mission 18 September 1944 (Courtesy of Dunkeswell Memorial Museum).

Crew 17 studying a patrol chart before the mission (Courtesy of Dunkeswell Memorial Museum).

Crew 17 VB-110 collecting flying gear from the locker room. Pictured are W.J. Hollis (AMM2c), M.M Joy (AMM3c), A.J. Tatum (ARM3c), and W. Raven (S1c)(Courtesy of Dunkeswell Memorial Museum).

.50 caliber ammunition being prepared for the PB4Y-1's guns (Courtesy of Dunkeswell Memorial Museum).

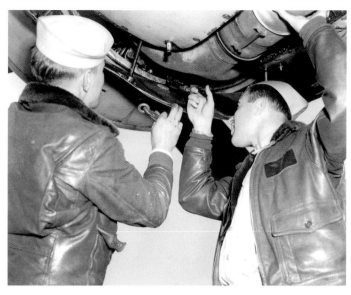

ARM Burfield and Lt. Greiwe perform an engine check before the mission (Courtesy of Dunkeswell Memorial Museum).

Checking the depth charges with the open bomb doors (Courtesy of Dunkeswell Memorial Museum).

and was later questioned about how he felt. Assigned to an area west of St. Nazaire, France in Liberator B-12Z (BurAer 63930), the crew encountered two fishing boats manned by German radio crews. Cohen ordered a strafing attack that caused one of the boats to sink and Wake remembered thinking that the remaining boat would pick up the survivors. After the debriefing, Cohen asked Wake, "Fred, I hope you do not have any misgivings about strafing the boat. They have been warned to stay out of the area." Wake replied, "No Sir, I do not, that is why I am here. It is my job."[57]

FAW-7 continued to become casualties of war. It really doesn't matter how an individual dies, everybody eventually reaches that point, but one wishes to prolong it as long as possible. Unfortunately, in war, which is a young person's vocation, an individual might not get a chance to prolong life and it really doesn't matter if a life is extinguished through enemy fire or as the result of an accident. A considerable number of FAW-7 Liberator crews met their fate through training accidents or while taking off or landing. Lieutenant (jg) John G. Byrnes and his crew from VB-110 met their fate on the night of 24 August 1944 during familiarization flight when their plane hit the top of Moel Seity Mountain near Brecon, in southern Wales. On 14 September, Lieutenant Trudeau while ferrying a PB4Y-1 from the United States was forced to ditch his plane because of fuel exhaustion, six miles off coast of Galway, Ireland. Four of Trudeau's men went down with the plane and another, S1c Nathan Beckwith, later died in the crew's life raft while awaiting rescue.

A waist gunner, possibly E.J. Griffin, checking his Browning .50 caliber machinegun before the patrol (Courtesy of Dunkeswell Memorial Museum).

Crew 17 of VB-110 on patrol. The pilot relaxes while the copilot takes over the controls (Courtesy of Dunkeswell Memorial Museum).

Averting Disaster

Each time a Liberator went out on patrol, it carried the means in which to destroy an enemy submarine. Typically, the aircraft's bomb bay housed a combination of general-purpose bombs, depth charges, and MK-24 *Zombies*. However, as most patrols didn't produce a submarine sighting, a plane often returned with its ordnance intact. After landing and parking the plane, Navy ordnance men came in to unload the bombs. It was during such a typical event in the life of a bombing squadron that Ralph M. Debevec, a member of squadron VPB-105; almost became another name etched on the Dunkeswell memorial plaque.

After returning from an uneventful patrol, Debevec and the rest of the crew commanded by Lieutenant (jg) McElroy headed to their huts for a few hours of sleep before returning to the plane and making a 120-hour maintenance check. Unbeknownst to the resting crew, the men charged with unloading the *Zombies* didn't show up for work that day.

Several hours later, the plane's crew arrived to do their part of the check up which included inspecting the bomb release mechanisms. Debevic climbed up into the bombardier station and began the three-step procedure of, first, opening the bomb bay doors, two, salvo all bomb racks, and three, check for proper functioning of individual bomb racks. The bomb bay doors opened and unknown to him at the time, "The men who were supposed to work in the bomb bay stared unbelievably at what was in the aircraft. They were so shocked they didn't move or make a sound." Instead of seeing an empty bomb bay, two Mk-24 *Zombies* were still attached to the bomb racks.

A waist gunner searches for submarines and enemy aircraft (Courtesy of Dunkeswell Memorial Museum).

The primary radioman tuning a BC-375D Transmitter (Courtesy of Dunkeswell Memorial Museum).

The navigator plots the plane's course over the Bay of Biscay (Courtesy of Dunkeswell Memorial Museum).

Crew 17 boards a truck for debriefing after the patrol (Courtesy of Dunkeswell Memorial Museum).

After the mission, the Plane Captain completes all the documents (Courtesy of Dunkeswell Memorial Museum).

Members of Crew 17 relaxing prior to the de-briefing (Courtesy of Dunkeswell Memorial Museum).

Men from Crew 17 wait in line outside of a telephone box in Dunkeswell Village. Left to right: S1c W Raven (in the box) ARM2c E.J. Griffin, ARM1c, E.R. Burfield, AMM1c E.E. Stoner AOM2c, and D.H. Noddin (Courtesy of Dunkeswell Memorial Museum).

Debevec, still inside the bombardier station, performed the next step in the check out procedure of salvoing the bomb racks and that's when all hell broke loose as the two *Zombies* left inside the plane came crashing down to the ground. Immediately, all hands broke and ran from the aircraft. Meanwhile, Debevec couldn't see what was going on but he heard the sound of the crash, followed by shouts, and profanity.

Looking out the small bombardier's window, he could see men running in all directions. Debevec didn't know what was going on but decided to head aft to check the situation. He crawled through the empty radio compartment and then through the empty bomb

bay. There wasn't anybody around. Looking down, he saw the *Zombies*, which were never to be left unguarded, and were always unloaded first after a mission, on the ground. He realized that if they were going to explode they would have done so by then. He looked up at the safety wires still fastened to the bomb racks on one end and the other end still holding the pins that were pulled from the nose contact fuse making the homing torpedoes armed. The *Zombies* were armed but the height of the bomb racks to the ground wasn't quite high enough to permit the nose fuse from making contact with the pavement. Hence, no explosion. However, before the accidental release, two sailors had been arguing about whether or

Members of Crew 17 meet local inhabitants of Dunkeswell during off duty (Courtesy of Dunkeswell Memorial Museum).

PB4Y-1 Liberator "J" 231 of VB-114 before taking off on a night patrol on 11 August 1944. The plane was airborne at 2008 hours and returned at 0529 hours on 12 August (Courtesy of Dunkeswell Memorial Museum).

A Spanish fishing boat spotted by Liberator B-103 of VPB-103 on 22 April 1945. The fishing boats were suspected of passing information to the Germans on the location of American and British search planes (see the leaflets dropped onto them) (Courtesy of Dunkeswell Memorial Museum).

Conformément à nos AVER-TISSEMENTS REPETES, il est absolument indispensable que vous vous éloigniez sans aucun délai de ces lieux de pêche

Peut-être certains d'entre vous savent déjà que nous avons été obligés, bien malgré nous, d'employer la force pour assurer le succès des opérations.

Il y a pour vous DANGER DE MORT. Choisissez immédiate-ment entre deux solutions :

(1) Ou bien regagner à l'instant même votre port d'attache;

(2) Ou bien rallier un port anglais. **Dans ce cas arborez un pavillon blanc ou un signal blanc à votre mât de misaine.**

F.132

not the plane's tires had proper pressure, it seemed they didn't. But, if the tires had been properly inflated the nose fuse would have had enough room to make contact and detonate. Its all relative, sometimes a millisecond or a fraction of an ounce makes a difference between life and death.[58]

Operations Reduced

Beginning on 1 October 1944, the designation for U.S. Navy bombing squadrons changed with the "VB" code changing to "VPB" for Navy Patrol and Bombing squadrons. Although the patrols continued negative for a considerable length of time, U-boat activity didn't cease and it remained a constant threat to Allied shipping throughout the entire Atlantic area. Consequently, the increased use of the schnorkel by U-boats caused FAW-7 and Coastal Command squadrons to depend on the use of radar and sonobouys. Although buoys were dropped on 16 disappearing radar contacts during the months of October, November, and December, there were no successful attacks.

Because of poor weather conditions, which increased the number of delays in take-offs from Dunkeswell, many of the sorties during December 1944 took off from St. Eval with planes being flown to that airfield the night before a mission to effect early morning departures. However, this procedure proved unsatisfactory and

Translation of leaflets dropped on French and Spanish fishing vessels by FAW-7 aircraft:
Consistent with our repeated warnings, it is absolutely essential that you depart and stay away from these fishing waters immediately
Perhaps some among you already know that whether we wish to or not we must use force in order to assure the success of our missions or operations.
You are in DANGER OF DEATH. Choose immediately between these two solutions:
1   Either return to your home port.
2   Or put into an English port, in this case, hoist a white flag or signal on your foremast. (Translation by Molly Reedy Baker. Photograph courtesy of Dunkeswell Memorial Museum).

A crew from VB-114 in the briefing room at U.S.N.A.F. Dunkeswell on 11 August 1944 Top front row: Harry Kirkland, Oren Clark, Don Williams, Meya Minchin, Edward Ellwood, Joe Bunting, and unknown. Second row (from the top): First three unknown Tom Keady and unknown. Under the window (from the top): first four unknown, Ray DeYoung, and last two unknown (Courtesy of Dunkeswell Memorial Museum).

Inspection by Commander George C. Miller Commanding Officer, N.A.F. Dunkeswell, inspects enlisted personnel on 9 September 1944 (Courtesy of Dunkeswell Memorial Museum).

was abandoned after 31 December. Moreover, operations were hampered for several weeks when the main runway at Dunkeswell was resurfaced. Consequently, the planes scheduled to go on operational missions the next day were flown to a former R.A.F. base at Upottery, with a light load of gasoline, the afternoon before the mission. After patrols were completed, flight crews were taken by truck back to Dunkeswell to spend the night. They were awakened an hour earlier the next morning to allow time for the truck ride back to the planes at Upottery. In January 1945, the airfield became the base of operations for two additional PB4Y-1 squadrons, VPB-107 and 112.

It was a frustrating existence. The frustration of flying out of an airfield that was routinely socked in due to weather and the ceaseless number of long, uneventful patrols conducted by FAW-7 Liberator crews was summed up in the squadron history of VPB-105 penned soon after the war. From 1 December 1944 until May 1945, the squadron flew three to four daily missions of 10 or 13 hours duration, in all the weather that only England could create. During this period, intensive day and night training in searchlights, detection of schnorkel, and anti-submarine bombing, was carried out. Despite all this effort, not a single established U-boat contact was made. Yet, with or without successful attacks on submarines, squadrons such as VPB-105 provided valuable reinforcements for Coastal Command's war against the U-boat and, as 1945 dawned, the clock began ticking down to victory in Europe.

Boarding a PB4Y-1 and preparing to head back to the United States on 14 July 1944 (Courtesy of Dunkeswell Memorial Museum).

Happy day for Charely Lindstedt and his crew as they prepare to return to the United States on 14 July 1944 (Courtesy of Charley Lindstedt via Dunkeswell Memorial Museum).

Photograph of VB-103 Crew 11 during May 1944. Back row (left to right): Lyle G. VanHook (AMM1c), Ensign Bruce E. Spilker (navigator), Lt. Richard L. Thrum (PPC), Ensign Abraham Genderson (co-pilot), and Rex L. McCoy (AMM2c). Front row (left to right): C.A. Sacharczuk (S2c), John F. Ciliberto (AMM3c), James P. O'Neill (S1c), Julian O. Pierce (AOM2c), and George L. McLean (ARM3c). Trum, VanHook, Rex McCoy, and Julian Pierce were veterans of VB-112 and survived a ditching of their Liberator off Portugal on 30 November 1943 (Courtesy of Gene McIntyre).

Lt. Oren Clark and crew of VB-114 Dunkeswell in August 1944 (Courtesy of Dunkeswell Memorial Museum).

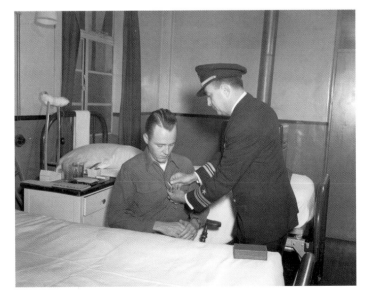

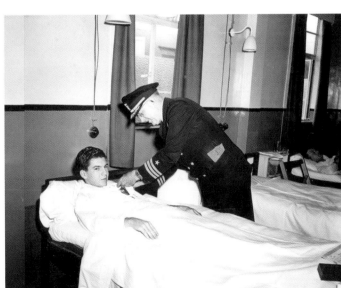

Lt. Commander H.W. King, Executive Officer FAW-7, awarding a Purple Heart at the base hospital in August 1944 (Courtesy of Dunkeswell Memorial Museum).

Commander George Miller in the base hospital in August 1944 presenting a Purple Heart Medal to a member of FAW-7 wounded in action (Courtesy of Dunkeswell Memorial Museum).

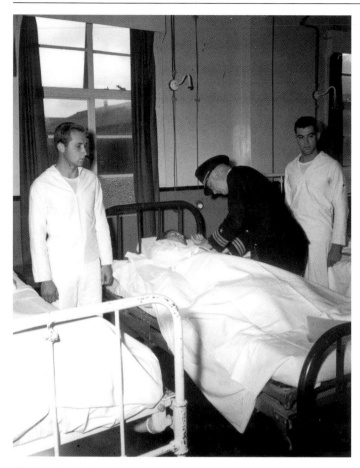

Commander Miller presenting Purple Heart awards at the hospital on 27 July 1944. (Courtesy of Dunkeswell Memorial Museum).

Commander Miller congratulating AMM2c E. B. Birdsong (U.S.N.R.), after being presented with a Purple Heart (Courtesy of Dunkeswell Memorial Museum).

Commander G. C. Miller inspects the Commissary Section of FAW-7 on 9 September 1944. There were very few opportunities for African Americans in the U.S. Navy during World War II and they were not allowed to serve with aircrews (Courtesy of Dunkeswell Memorial Museum).

PB4Y-1 "H" B-8 of VB-103 (BurAer 32200) on 6 September 1944. She was stricken on 9 December 1944 after skidding on a wet runway (Courtesy of Dunkeswell Memorial Museum).

PB4Y-1 "C" B-3 of VB-110 (BurAer 63921) over Dunkeswell Control Tower Sept 1944. (NARA 80-G 282277 Courtesy of National Archives via Dunkeswell Memorial Museum).

Navy construction workers lay a new runway at Dunkeswell (Courtesy of Dunkeswell Memorial Museum).

Navy construction site at Dunkeswell on 19 October 1944 (Courtesy of Dunkeswell Memorial Museum).

Crew 5 VB/VPB-114 during October 1944. Standing (left to right): Chief Radioman A. Bardakos, Ensign Cecil D. Jones, Ensign Grover B. Cobb, Lt. (jg) J.C. Routh, Lt. Edward Watson, and Joe Germana. Front row (left to right) ARM3c F.G. Butterfield, ARM3c R. Goetz, AOM3c Earl Slankard, AMM2c 'Sonny' E.W. Duncan, AOM3c Haskel Ingpam, and AMM1c Leroy C. Seitz. Not included "Bo" Manning ARM2/c (Courtesy of Dunkeswell Memorial Museum).

Six's Avenger (BurAer 38751), a VB-105 Liberator, was flown to Clinton, Oklahoma after the war where it was scrapped (Courtesy of Eugene B. Shea).

PATSU checks PB4Y-1 (BurAer 63944) during November 1944. The plane belonged to Crew 7B of VB/VPB-105 (Courtesy of Dunkeswell Memorial Museum).

Crew 9 of VB-114 (Courtesy of Dunkeswell Memorial Museum).

Men leaving N.A.F. Dunkeswell in December 1944 (Courtesy of Dunkeswell Memorial Museum).

B-17 Flying Fortresses of the 571ˢᵗ Bombing Squadron, 390ᵗʰ Bomb Group, U.S.A.A.F. lined up at Dunkeswell on 13 December 1944. They had to land at Dunkeswell because of bad weather on the return trip from a raid on Germany (Courtesy of Dunkeswell Memorial Museum).

Candy, fresh fruit, and canned goods collected for the children of Dunkeswell by the men of FAW-7 for the 1944 Christmas party (Courtesy of Dunkeswell Memorial Museum).

Captain George C. Miller at the Christmas party for local children on 21 December 1944 (Courtesy of Dunkeswell Memorial Museum).

Quonset huts and snow at Dunkeswell during the winter of 1944-45 (Courtesy of Dunkeswell Memorial Museum).

"Santa Claus" giving a hand-made toy to a local child during Christmas 1944 (Courtesy of Dunkeswell Memorial Museum).

"Santa Claus" and American sailors enjoying the Christmas spirit (Courtesy of Dunkeswell Memorial Museum).

Local children sing Christmas songs at N.A.F. Dunkeswell (Courtesy of Dunkeswell Memorial Museum).

Singing Christmas songs during the Christmas party on 21 December 1944 (Courtesy of Dunkeswell Memorial Museum).

"Santa's Helpers" who built toys for the local children brought back memories to the men who were far from home (Courtesy of Dunkeswell Memorial Museum).

Christmas Mass for men of the Dunkeswell Air Group on 21 December 1944. They didn't know it at the time, but this would be their last Christmas in England (Courtesy of Dunkeswell Memorial Museum).

PB4Y-1 "O" B-15 of VPB-103 (BurAer 38784) piloted by Lt. C.M. Weyland crashed due to ice on the runway, 27 December 1944 (Courtesy of Dunkeswell Memorial Museum).

7

Victory and the Demise of FAW-7

I remember they all disappeared almost overnight!
-Mike Jarrett on the Americans
leaving Dunkeswell after the war.

As 1945 dawned, searchlight training began and a few of the Wing's Liberators were fitted with the Leigh Light. Night practices soon followed with day and night practice runs being made on American PT-Boats from Motor Torpedo Boat Squadron 35 in Lyme Bay, and eventually the British provided a live submarine equipped with a dummy schnorkel for exercises off Brest Peninsula. Additionally, a couple of night searchlight missions were flown without success.

The work of the Dunkeswell Air Group intensified during the last few months of the war as U-boats made a last ditch effort to break out into the Atlantic and attack shipping from their bases in Norway. On New Year's Day 1945, Lieutenant Dwight D. Nott of VPB-103 sighted a small compact quantity of bluish white smoke above the surface of the water.

One of the crewmember's was "Dick" Alsop—who joined the Navy in June 1942 at 17. Prior to joining VPB-10 he flew with VB-130, a PV-1 Ventura Squadron, which flew ASW in the Caribbean. On this particular mission, "We had been on patrol for several hours and could spend but a short period in the area. The crew laid a sonobuoy pattern, which gave positive results and four frigates were homed into the area. They confirmed the presence of a submarine and made two attacks, which proved unsuccessful.[59]

Records do not indicate a submarine being lost on the date and location specified. However, there was now some tangible proof in the minds of the flight personnel of the appearance and operating affects of sohnorkeling submarines, which had been drilled into them for several months. Lieutenant Nott's crew would get another chance at a U-boat during April 1945, which proved to be the last successful attack carried out by a FAW-7 Liberator crew.

Commander Joe Bettens, skipper of VPB-103 during 1945 (Courtesy of Dunkeswell Memorial Museum).

Lt. Commander Brewer new Executive officer for VPB-103(Courtesy of Dunkeswell Memorial Museum).

U.S.N.A.F. Satellite Base Upottery looking east on 11 April 1945. Upottery was a satellite of Dunkeswell when the runways at Dunkeswell were being repaired. Beginning in January 1945, two new squadrons consisting of VPB-107 and 112 were based there to supplement the strength of FAW-7 (Courtesy of Dunkeswell Memorial Museum).

Arrival of VPB-107 and 112

Winter 1945 at Dunkeswell turned out to be the worst on record for the region causing 50 of VPB-103's missions to be cancelled. The coldest weather recorded in the area in 75 years was chalked up one night, and the countryside was blanketed in three feet of snow for a period of about two weeks. At one time, no planes took off for four days because of ice and snow on the runways. Because of foul weather, operational accidents continued taking the lives of more men. Diverting to another airfield due to weather led to four deaths

on 3 January when Lieutenant George Pantano of VPB-105, flew into Beacon Hill while making an approach to the Royal Air Force field at Exeter, Devon. The deaths of Pantano and his crew were the last suffered by the Dunkeswell Air Group in Great Britain.

Increased U-boat activity in the Bay of Biscay raised enough concern with the Commander, U.S. Fleet that he ordered 2 PB4Y-1 squadrons and a detachment of MAD equipped PBY-5A's of VP-63 for temporary duty with FAW-7. VPB-107, responsible for the destruction of five U-boats between 1943 and 1945 while serving

Upottery Airfield shortly before D-Day 1944 when it was being used as a staging area. Note all the gliders dispersed around the airfield. The U.S. Army's 101st Airborne Division left from here (Courtesy of Dunkeswell Memorial Museum).

VB-105 Crew next to PB4Y-1 "V" taken on 24 February 1945. One of the men has been identified as William E. Swan, back row 2nd from left (Courtesy of Dunkeswell Memorial Museum).

Rear Admiral McFall at an award ceremony. He was the second and last Commanding Officer of FAW-7 and served in that capacity between 31 March and 2 August 1945 (Courtesy of Dunkeswell Memorial Museum).

PB4Y-1 "E" No. 85 of VPB-112 running up engines at Upottery Airfield (Courtesy of Dunkeswell Memorial Museum).

VPB-114 Crew 9 Enlisted men. Top (left to right): Don Anderson, Jerry Brotherson, Nick Haiden, and Willie Weaver. Bottom (left to right): Pete Wardell, Al Flory, and Woody Woodard (Courtesy of Dunkeswell Memorial Museum).

Green Banana of VB-105 was being ferried back to the U.S. in January 1945 when it crashed into a mountain in French Morocco killing all on board. The crew in the photograph hasn't been identified (Courtesy of Eugene B. Shea).

with FAW-16 at Natal, Brazil, arrived in England on 7 January 1945.[60]

A week later, on the 13th, VPB-112 flew in from Port Lyautey. To base the new arrivals, FAW-7 established Air Group 2 at Upottery airfield five miles from Dunkeswell on 11 January and renamed it U.S.N. Satellite Air Field Upottery. The acquisition coincided with Lieutenant Commander Duncan A. Campbell assuming command of VPB-110. However, the new squadrons had to wait for operations to begin as flights were cancelled due to bad weather from 12 to 31 January.

VPB-112 operations finally began on 15 February 1945 with Lieutenants McGillivray and Benson flying the first uneventful missions over the English Channel. This was followed with VPB-107 becoming operational on the 22nd with Lieutenants Clark and Johnson flying that squadron's first missions. Less than two weeks later, VPB-112's contribution to the war against the U-boat transpired. During the late afternoon of 27 February, Lieutenant O. B. Denison in Liberator "H" (BurAer 38868) began investigating a moving oil slick 112 miles south of Wolf Rock off the English Coast. After notifying the base, Denison left to contact surface units of the

Crew 13 of VB/VPB-103 commanded by Lt. Miller, wearing the distinctive squadron insignia on their jackets. The men identified in this photograph are Kenderine (ARM3c) (bottom right), followed by Rivenbark (AOM3c), and J. Mahoney (AMM3c). Second left is McCosker (AOM3c) with J. Miller (ARM2c) (left), and Lt. Miller (top center) (Courtesy of Gene McIntyre).

VB-107 Duty Office, Upottery Field on 17 April 1945. From left to right: Mike Zelenock, Hudges, Bill Kohel, Fred Felkel, and David Sigler (Courtesy of Fred Felkel via Dunkeswell Memorial Museum).

Right: Lt. Dwight D. Nott in Liberator "K" of VPB-103 attacking the U-326 on 25 April 1945. A schnorkel (top left) and the impact of two MK-24 acoustic mines can be seen (Courtesy of Dunkeswell Memorial Museum).

Bottom left: The explosions of the MK-24 acoustic mines as they find the U-326 and detonate (Courtesy of Dunkeswell Memorial Museum).

Bottom right: Top left is a smoke marker, and in the right/middle center is an oil slick with a corpse rising to the surface marking U-326's grave (Courtesy of Dunkeswell Memorial Museum).

WE HOPE THAT YOU ENJOY THIS BOOK...and that it will occupy a proud place in your library. We would like to keep you informed about other publications from Schiffer Books.
Please return this card with your requests and comments. **(Please print clearly in ink.)**
Note: We don't share our mailing list with anyone.

Title of Book Purchased _____

☐ Purchased at: _____ ☐ received as a gift

Comments or ideas for books you would like to see us publish: _____

Your Name: _____

Address _____

City _____ State _____ Zip _____ Country _____

E-mail Address _____

Please provide your email address to receive announcements of new releases

☐ Please send me a **free** *Schiffer Antiques, Collectibles, & the Arts*
☐ Please send me a **free** *Schiffer Woodcarving, Woodworking, and Crafts Catalog*
☐ Please send me a **free** *Schiffer Military, Aviation, and Automotive History Catalog*
☐ Please send me a *Schiffer Lifestyle, Design, and Body, Mind, & Spirit Catalog*

See our most current books on the web at **www.schifferbooks.com**
Contact us at: Phone: 610-593-1777; Fax: 610-593-2002; or E-mail: info@schifferbooks.com
SCHIFFER BOOKS ARE CURRENTLY AVAILABLE FROM YOUR BOOKSELLER

PLACE
STAMP
HERE

For the latest releases and
thousands of books in print,
fill out the back of this card
and return it today!

SCHIFFER PUBLISHING LTD
4880 LOWER VALLEY ROAD
ATGLEN, PA 19310-9717 USA

Site 4
England

Jack Wellinghurst at VPB-103's Site-4 shows off a newspaper's headline, Victory in Europe (VE-Day). Within weeks the men of Dunkeswell were heading home (Courtesy of Jack Wellinghurst via Dunkeswell Memorial Museum).

Crew 5 of VPB-103 in May 1945 after receiving medals for the sinking of the U-326 on 25 April 1945. From left to right: Lt. Dwight Nott, Patrol Plane Commander, Distinguished Flying Cross; Lt. (jg) Kenneth Robinson, Co-pilot, Air Medal; Lt. (jg) John S Walker, Navigator, Air Medal; R.H. Roberts, Plane Captain, Air Medal; J.B. Jones, Second Radioman, Air Medal; Renfro Pace, Waist gunner, Air Medal; Joseph Kirchdorfer, Tail gunner, Air Medal; Robert Mayer, Nose gunner, Air Medal. Missing from the picture are Marco Vaccher, Waist gunner, Air Medal, and Richard Alsop, First Radioman, Air Medal (Courtesy of Dunkeswell Memorial Museum).

2nd Escort Group about the oil slick by using a blinker light. Below the surface, the submerged U-327, a type VIIC/41 submarine, was on her third patrol under the command of *Kapitänleutnant* Hans Lemcke.

Returning to the area, Denison had his men drop dye markers some 100 feet ahead of the slick, which moved up to the dye and passed it in about two minutes. Denison radioed to base, "Positive contact," and then made a run up the trail of oil. A schnorkel was seen rising out of the water about four feet before it submerged. However, the plane had moved beyond the target before a depth charge attack could be made. Since, the Liberator carried no sonobouys an attack would have been futile and so Denison left the submarine to the rapidly approaching 2nd Escort Group, which took care of the U-327 and her crew of 46.

Attacks on the U-681 and U-326
By March 1945, with the enemy's situation on the Continent deteriorating rapidly, Coastal Command called on the squadrons for extra alertness and diligence in their patrol work. After the successful attack on the U-327, a month went by before another attack was made against Germany's silent service by a PB4Y-1. Lieutenant R.N. Field on 12 March, of VPB-103, spotted the fully surfaced U-681, a type VIIC boat, under the command of *Oberleutnant zur See* Werner Gebauer. Southwest of the Scilly Islands, a set of five small islands 28 miles off Lands End, England, the submarine had run aground while attempting to enter St. Mary's, damaging her hull and screws. Gebauer managed to bring the U-681 to the surface but it wouldn't dive, a very dangerous predicament. Therefore, the U-boat's captain decided that the safest bet was to head for Ireland

Bunting on Living Quarters in celebration of VE-Day (Courtesy of Jack Wellinghurst via Dunkeswell Memorial Museum).

U-boats U-249 (top) and U-825 (bottom) surrendering to a PB4Y-1 (Courtesy of Dunkeswell Memorial Museum).

U.S. Navy personnel inspect U-1023 at Plymouth on 31 May 1945. This U-boat surrendered to allied forces at Weymouth on 10 May 1945 (Courtesy of Dunkeswell Memorial Museum).

After the war, it was time to think of the future and here is the wedding of Joan Kathleen Atyeo of Weston Super Mare on 26 May 1945 to John Samuel Walker who was stationed at Dunkeswell. Front row (left to right): John Walker, Joan Walker, Dwight Nott (Best man), and Lee Howells (Bridesmaid and sister to bride). Back row (left to right): unknown, Stan May, Kenneth Robinson, John Morrow, Joe Glab, and unknown. All officers were with VPB-103 and Dwight Nott and Kenneth Robinson were in Crew 5 with John Walker (Courtesy of Dunkeswell Memorial Museum).

and internment. Gebauer and his crew didn't get the chance as Field's bomber came in low and fast, dropping a string of eight depth charges. The concussion from the explosions began flooding the boat and Gebauer decided to abandon ship. Of the U-681's 49 crewmembers, 38 managed to pile into dinghies while demolition charges were set and main the vents opened. As the American aircrew and the German submariners watched, the submarine slipped beneath the waves. Lieutenant Field was awarded the British Distinguished Flying Cross on 30 March 1945.[61]

On 25 April, VPB-103's Crew 5 led by Lieutenant Dwight D. Nott, who made an unsuccessful attack in January, got his second chance when he sighted and attacked a schnorkeling submarine while on patrol southwest of the Brest Peninsula. It was the U-326, a Type VIIC boat under the command of *Oberleutnant zur See* Peter Matthes. On board the Liberator was "Dick" Alsop. "Our crew got in 43 missions at Dunkeswell. There were those long 24 hour duty stretches from Ops Chow (dining before and after a mission) to the briefing, loading the equipment, getting air borne, complet-

No longer useful, PB4Y-1's that were considered obsolete were abandoned at Dunkeswell and broken up after VE-Day (Courtesy of Dunkeswell Memorial Museum).

PB4Y-1 "P" No. 95 in the process of being broken up (Courtesy of Dunkeswell Memorial Museum).

ing the patrol, debriefing, Ops Chow again, unloading the plane, and then secure until noon the next day. That is, if everything went according to plan, which it didn't."

At 1938 hours, the co-pilot Lieutenant (jg) Robinson and R. L. Page, AOM3c, starboard waist gunner looked out, and sighted a schnorkel at a distance of two miles. The aircraft was flying at 800 feet and Lieutenant Nott immediately chopped the throttles and started a turn to starboard in order to deliver an attack. Nott sharpened his turn to starboard, keeping the target in view, at the same time reducing speed and altitude in order to set up for an attack. The schnorkel continued on the same course and speed, apparently not aware of the aircraft' a presence.

The Liberator's approach and attack took place at 1940 hours, two minutes after sighting the U-boat, and two Mk-24 *Zombies* were dropped with maximum intervalometer setting of 150 feet at an altitude of 200 feet. After the torpedoes were away, a straight

heading was continued for 20 seconds before Lieutenant Nott made a turn to starboard for a return heading to the point of impact. While the Liberator turned, the torpedoes were seen to hone in on direction of the submarine and a moment later, a large explosion was seen and the schnorkel was seen to jump five feet into the air and then disappear. Alsop remembers dropping the sonobouys to track the submarine's path, "just a few seconds too late to pick up the sub's engine sounds but we did record a significant amount of under water breaking up noises. At least that is what the Navy intelligence people in D.C. determined after they heard the tape. There was no chance for survivors."

After circling explosion for several minutes, Lieutenant Nott and his crew continued sowing a standard 1,550-yard sonobouy pattern, which was completed at 1954 hours. At 2015 hours, an oil patch extending over an area of 150 yards in diameter was seen approximately 250 yards south southwest of the position of the ex-

The broken and twisted remains of a PB4Y-1 that once flew over the Bay of Biscay and the English Channel (Courtesy of Dunkeswell Memorial Museum).

In the foreground are the remains of an R.A.F. Coastal Command Liberator. In the rear is a tailless PB4Y-1 waiting to be broken up (Courtesy of Dunkeswell Memorial Museum).

plosion. The men aboard the U-326 had met their fate and the Dunkeswell Air Group had made its last kill. Lieutenant Nott received the DFC while Alsop and the rest of the crew were awarded the Air Medal. In June 1945, after returning to the United States, Alsop rejoined a Navy PV-1 Squadron, this time VPB-143.[62]

Victory

With Germany's unconditional surrender on 8 May 1945, U-boats were ordered to surrender to the nearest port. In the sky, Dunkeswell Air Group planes were informed to be on the lookout for such vessels. On 9 May, Lieutenant F. L. Schaum of VPB-110 and Lieutenant D. P. Housh of VPB-112 accepted the surrender of *Kapitänleutnant* Uwe Kock's U-249, the first to surrender to a PB4Y-1. A day later, a fully surfaced U-516 commanded by *Oberleutnant* Gerhard Stoelker surrendered to Lieutenant Edward K. Gleason in aircraft "B" and Lieutenant S.T. Gillmor of VPB-112 without a shot being fired. On same day, U-825 surrendered to 112's Lieutenant L. A. Murch. On the 15th Lieutenant John L. Thafte of VPB-105 was diverted from his mission to *Kapitänleutnant* Lothar Martin's U-776, which had radioed its desire to surrender and Thafte escorted the U-boat until surface vessels appeared.

While Dunkeswell and Upottery-based Liberators were accepting the surrender of German submarines, photo-reconnaissance missions and security patrols continued through 28 May 1945 when the orders to cease operations was given by Coastal Command. With victory in Europe there was no longer a need for antisubmarine squadrons and, within a couple of weeks, Air Group 1 and Air Group

2 received orders to return home. The men packed their bags, collected the souvenirs they had acquired while in England and waited for transportation that would carry them back to the United States and their waiting loved ones. However, they wouldn't be leaving the way they arrived, on board a lumbering PB4Y-1 Liberators, instead, most departed Britain by ship. The planes, the ones that had served the aircrews well for nearly two years, were turned over to the Headquarters Squadron. The disposition and fate, preordained by the advancement of aeronautics, would send many to the welder's torch.

VPB-103 personnel received orders on 4 June to board the U.S.S. *Unimai* at Bristol, England. The trip home was uneventful except for considerable number of men coming down with seasickness. On 14 June, the ship arrived at Norfolk, Virginia where 30-day leaves were granted. The squadron reformed on 4 August at Naval Air Station Crows Landing, California and immediately started an intensive ground and flight training program in the Consolidated-Vultee PB4Y-2 Privateer, a single-tail sister of the Liberator. The intention was to reform for future deployment to the Pacific after two months training. Yet, the fortunes of war cancelled plans with the surrender of Japan. Without a combat role, the squadron was decommissioned at Naval Air Station, Alameda, California, on 31 August 1945.

As for VPB-105, Lieutenant Commander John K. Sloatman, with the squadron since May 1943, became the new skipper. Two crews, which had picked up new planes in the United States and were enroute to England, were recalled when Germany surrendered

The Stars and Stripes is lowered as the R.A.F. ensign is raised marking the handing over of Dunkeswell N.A.F. by the U.S. Navy to the R.A.F. in August 1945 (Courtesy of Dunkeswell Memorial Museum).

A bugler plays taps during the first Memorial Day Service held in 1945 in remembrance to the men of FAW-7 who died during the Second World War (Courtesy of Dunkeswell Memorial Museum).

The Memorial Day Service in 1945 (Courtesy of Dunkeswell Memorial Museum).

and transferred to Headquarters Squadron 52. Shortly after the surrender, the squadron was authorized to fly sightseeing tours of the invasion coast, from the Normandy Peninsula to Holland, and twenty-five miles inland. Normandy, which became the final resting-place for thousands of Allied and German soldiers, had become a tourist attraction. Ground personnel were given priority as passengers on these flights and, on 30 May 1945, an overnight excursion flight to Paris was made, taking seven officers and fifteen enlisted men. Between 3 and 4 June, three contingents of the squadron left Great Britain via the ships *Albermarle*, *Rehoboth*, and *Unimak*. VPB-105 arrived in the United States nine days later and was decommissioned on 27 June 1945.

Lieutenant Commander Campbell's VPB-110 departed England on 4 June 1945 aboard the *Albernarle* and arrived in the United States on the 14th. The squadron was scheduled for reforming on 15 September to begin training with the PB4Y-2 Privateer. However, with Japan's capitulation, the squadron was decommissioned on 1 September.

The last PB4Y-1 Liberator of FAW-7 departed Dunkeswell on 26 July 1945 with most going to the Naval Air Station in Clinton, Oklahoma where they were later scrapped. FAW-7 relinquished control of Dunkeswell to the British in August 1945 and the R.A.F. continued using Dunkeswell until 1950 when most of it was sold to private investors. During its two years of operations in England between July 1943 and 31 May 1945, FAW-7 aircraft had accumulated 6, 464 operational sorties and flew 10, 581, 990 statute miles.

Epilogue:
Memories of Dunkeswell

In December 1945, St. Nicolas Church, with the assistance of the U.S. Embassy installed a Memorial Plaque listing names of U.S. Navy personnel that lost their lives while stationed at Dunkeswell. A memorial service is held annually the Sunday before Memorial Day and for appropriate special occasions. The Americans left but they were not forgotten as they left a mark on the rural English countryside. The United States Navy PB4Y-1 Squadrons which served in England are still remembered by the civilians.

Michael Jarrett remembers being a teenager when the "Yanks" operated from Dunkeswell. "My brother and I used to visit together but I was usually on my own. I was just one of those annoying children who used to gain unauthorized access to the airfield and have to be chased out by the Shore Police.

One summer, probably 1944, I was talking to one of the seamen at the Communal site when he told me it was a pity I wasn't there a bit earlier as there had been ice-cream in the Ship's store that afternoon. I suppose the disappointment must have shown, because he said to me to hang on…and he would see what he could find. They were all so kind to us children and generous. A few minutes later he came back with a large tin of pineapple juice, which he gave to me.

I was excited about this because we hadn't seen anything like this for nearly five years. The rations we got were frugal but adequate to live on. There were no luxuries! I was advised to put it into my saddlebag and take it home. The tin had no paper label like they have today, but was stenciled all around the circumference with "U.S. Navy Property." It must have been repeated several hundred times on the can!

I took it home and it was treated like a "prize of war." My Mum had it prominently displayed for all visitors to see. It really was a case of "see what I've got." The silly thing about this episode was, I don't even remember drinking it!"

On another occasion, Mike came face to face with a PB4Y-1 preparing to take off from the airfield. "I was cycling around the perimeter track when I met a PB4Y-1 coming towards me! The wing span was such that the wing tips were exactly as wide as the track and I wondered what I should do. I froze, and then watched as this plane came nearer and nearer. Luckily for me, it turned onto the main runway just 50 yards from me.

I just watched as the pilot did his checking, etc and ran the Pratt & Whitney engines faster and faster as he did the magneto checks etc. After several minutes the planes engines were run up to peak revs and this is the bit I remember most vividly, the prop tips were going so fast they went supersonic and made a noise like a whip cracking. While all this was happening I was aware of the whole airframe vibrating and everything looked so flimsy. When

St. Mary's Church flying the flag of the United States during Memorial Day 2000 (Courtesy of Dunkeswell Memorial Museum).

An aerial view of Dunkeswell Airfield in 2000 (Courtesy of Dunkeswell Memorial Museum).

the plane had been held against the brakes for a minute or so, the brakes were let off and I imagined with all that power on, it was going to gallop down the runway very fast. The reality was quite a contrast. The plane lumbered down the runway at a very low speed. Half way down the main runway was a dip of several feet and except the tail fins it completely went out of sight, only to reappear a bit further down the runway still firmly attached to the asphalt. It was only in the last few feet the plane staggered off the ground."[63]

Children, and to an extent adults, no matter where they live, have a tendency to collect objects they happen to find. The youngsters who grew up watching American bombers taking off and landing at Dunkeswell were no exception as Mike Jarrett reflected. "We also made quite a collection of general war materiel; a machine gun barrel, oxygen cylinders, ammunition, ammunition boxes, trays and many more things than I can remember!"

Then came Victory in Europe "VE" DAY. Hitler had been defeated and the war was over. For quite a long time after the war, the airfield was completely abandoned. Children would play inside a burnt fuselage of a PB4Y-1 left after the Navy had left. It was such a disappointment to us kids that the planes and men had gone."[64]

In the town of Dunkeswell, life slowly went back to normal. The children who watched PB4Y-1 Liberators take off and land during the war grew up, obtained jobs, married, and had children of

This is the memorial organ inside St. Mary's Church, Dunkeswell, donated by members of Fleet Air Wing 7 in memory of their fallen comrades (Courtesy of Dunkeswell Memorial Museum).

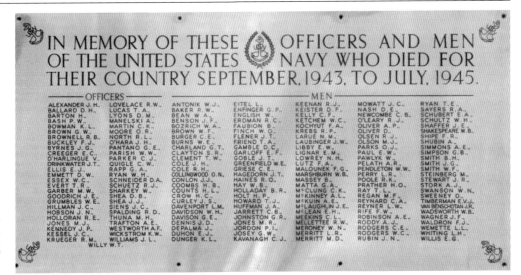

IN MEMORY OF THESE OFFICERS AND MEN OF THE UNITED STATES NAVY WHO DIED FOR THEIR COUNTRY SEPTEMBER, 1943, TO JULY, 1945.

OFFICERS

ALEXANDER J. H.
BALLARD D. H.
BARTON H.
BASH P. W.
BOWMAN K. L.
BROWN G. W.
BROWNELL R. B.
BUCKLEY F. J.
BYRNES J. G.
CREEGER E. C.
D'HARLINGUE V.
DRINKWATER J. T.
ELLIS E. J.
EMMETT D. W.
ESSEX W. C.
EVERT T. R.
GARBER M. W.
GOODRICH J. E.
GRUMBLES W. E.
HILLMAN J. C.
HOBSON J. N.
HOLLORAN R. E.
JONES M. J.
KENNEDY J. P.
KESSEL J. C.
KRUEGER R. M.

LOVELACE R. W.
LUCAS T. A.
LYONS D. M.
MANELSKI A.
MARTIN C. K.
MOORE O. R.
NORTH R. L.
O'HARA J. H.
PANTANO G. E.
PARISH W. W.
PARKER C. J.
QUIGLE C. W.
RAPP G. A.
RYAN W. H.
SCHNEIDER D. A.
SCHUETZ R. J.
SHARKEY W.
SHEA D. B.
SHEA J. J.
SIENS J. C.
SPALDING R. D.
THUNA M. H.
TRAFTON A. E.
WESTWORTH A. F.
WICKSTROM K. W.
WILLIAMS J. L.
WILLY W. T.

MEN

ANTONIK W. J.
BAKER R. W.
BEAN W. A.
BENSON J. F.
BOZRICH W. A.
BROWN W. F.
BURGER C. E.
BURNS W. E.
CHARLAND G. T.
CLAYTON S. R.
CLEMENT T. W.
COLE J. A.
COLE R. H.
COLLINGWOOD D. N.
CONLON J. J.
COOMBS H. B.
COUNTS H. L.
CROW H. C.
CURLEY J. S.
DAVENPORT L. M.
DAVIDSON W. H.
DAVISON G. E.
DENNIS J. D.
DEPALMA J.
DUHON E. J.
DUNGER K. L.

EITEL L.
ENFINGER G. P.
ENGLISH W. J.
ERDMAN R. C.
FAUBION B.
FINCH W. O.
FLENER J. T.
FRIEND T. A.
GAMBLE D. C.
GARLOFF E. F.
GOBLE J. T.
GREENFIELD W. E.
GRIESE C. E.
HAGEDORN J. T.
HAINES R. O.
HAY W. E.
HOLLADAY B. R.
HOLT H. P.
HOWARD T. J.
HUFFMAN J. C.
JARRETT C. B.
JOHNSTON G. R.
JONES M. R.
JORDON P. I.
JOSEY G. W.
KAVANAGH C. J.

KEENAN R. J.
KEISTER D. F.
KELLY C. F.
KETCHEM W. C.
KOCHYUT F. A.
KREBS R. P.
LARUE N. J.
LAUBINGER J. W.
LIBBY E. W.
LIGNAR E. M.
LOWREY N. H.
LUTZ F. A.
MALOUNEK F. G.
MARSHBURN W. B.
MASSEY B.
MATTA G. A.
McCLUNG C. K.
McKINNEY A. L.
McKUIN A. E.
McLAUGHLIN J. E.
McLEAN E. H.
MEEKINS C. L.
MELLETTEE R. W.
MERONEY W. N.
MERRITT L. R.
MERRITT M. D.

MOWATT J. C.
NASH D. E.
NEWCOMBE C. B.
O'LEARY R. J.
OLIVER A. P.
OLIVER D.
OLSEN R. J.
OLSON M. J.
PARKS O. J.
PAUL E. W.
PAWLYK W.
PELATH A. R.
PENDLETON W. W.
PERRY L. R.
POOLE R. K.
PRATHER H. O.
RAY T. L.
REGAN M. F.
REYNARD C. A.
REYNER L. W.
RIFE F. W.
ROBINSON A. E.
RODDY A. J.
RODGERS C. E.
RODGERS W. C.
RUBIN J. N.

RYAN T. E.
SAYERS R. A.
SCHUBERT E. A.
SCHULTZ W. H.
SHAFFER J. E.
SHAKESPEARE W. B.
SHIPE F. R.
SHUBIN J. A.
SIMMONS A. E.
SIMPSON G. B.
SMITH B. H.
SMITH J. G.
SMITH W. F.
STEINBERG M.
STEWART J. R.
STORK A. J.
SWANSON W. N.
SWEENEY D.
TIMBERMAN E. V. J.
VAN BENSCHOTAN J. R.
WADSWORTH W. B.
WAGNER J. F.
WALDRON F. J.
WEMETTE L. L.
WHITING L. H.
WILLIS E. G.

A memorial plaque inside the church inscribed with the names of the men who died while serving at Dunkeswell Naval Air Facility (Courtesy of Dunkeswell Memorial Museum).

their own. However, the airfield remained a permanent fixture in the community and it couldn't be ignored.

Dunkeswell Today

When the U.S. Navy left Dunkeswell in the summer of 1945 there was no immediate attempts, as one might imagine, commemorating the importance of the airfield, though in April 1946, there was a service inside the Dunkeswell church to mark the donation of an organ by the U.S. Navy. The airmen who did not return were also remembered on a plaque in the church. For many Navy veterans of FAW-7 civilian jobs, marriage, and children couldn't erase their service during the war. Time went by, the United States became embroiled in other conflicts, and the men of Mudville Heights grew older. Slowly, at first, during the 1950's, a veteran or two began making pilgrimages to Dunkeswell and reminisce. Over the years, the number of veterans crossing the Atlantic from their homes from across the United States steadily grew.

After 60 years, the airfield continues to be used by small aircraft, but most of the original World War II-era buildings fell into decay. It was only in 1985 that the first organized group of veterans

returned to Dunkeswell, by which time local people from another generation had established a temporary museum at the airfield. Because of those early efforts, the Dunkeswell Memorial Museum was opened in July 1997. Since then, the museum has become a focal point for veterans returning to the airfield and for families of lost airmen who, over fifty years later, were still trying to locate the place where their loved ones died. In one case a visitor wishing to commemorate her brother's death, laid flowers at the place near the end of the runway where local people knew her brother's plane had crashed.

The Trustees of the Dunkeswell Memorial Museum have a vision to create a "virtual war-time operation's experience including interactive exhibits, simulations, multi-media displays, special effects, artifacts donated by veterans and excavated from the site, photographic and documentation archive, and educational facilities. More recently, there has been a fear that some of the surviving installations at Dunkeswell may be demolished. The Ministry of Defense still owns installations at Dunkeswell, but the English Heritage Foundation is closely involved in assessing the status and future of important buildings. Unfortunately, they were not built to

Rear Admiral James Reedy, former commanding officer of VB-110, speaking at the Fatal Echo Memorial Ceremony on 18 August 1990 (Courtesy of Gene McIntyre).

The phone booth that appears in the Crew 17 sequence in Chapter 5 as it looks today (Courtesy of Bernard Stevens via Dunkeswell Memorial Museum).

Gene McIntyre, a veteran of VB-103, attending the 2000 FAW-7 Reunion (Courtesy of Gene McIntyre).

last for centuries and are in a state of decay. As of 2001, historic installations at the airfield have been recognized by enough people to stave off demolition or development. Existing structures under considered for restoration and development include the Administrative/Operations Complex and the control tower.[65]

The Veterans of Dunkeswell
James R. "Dick" Alsop was discharged from Navy in January 1946. After the war, he earned a BS Degree in Chemistry from Austin Peay College in May 1950. Afterward, he worked for U.S. Army Ordnance, Pfizer Corporation, and taught Junior High. As of this writing, he hasn't retired and currently works with his son's architectural/engineering firm.[66]

Lieutenant Bruce Enloe's life was cut short when he was one of 42 passengers killed in a commercial airliner crash in Florida in 1963. A park, the George Enloe Park in Anoka, Minnesota was dedicated in his honor. His former bombardier, Dallas Jones said during the park's dedication ceremony, "George left footprints on the sands of time. His story should be an incentive for anyone who doubts they can do what they are striving to do. George Albert Enloe is a hero today. He will always be a hero to the city of Aoka for dedicating this park to his memory."[67]

Commander L. E. Harmon, the third commanding officer for VB-105, advanced to the rank of Captain and served as Commander of an AEW Wing during the early 1960s.

Charles Knauff left the Navy in May 1945 and then spent three years running a service station in Birmingham, Alabama before re-

turning to his family farm in Ohio for five years. After being injured in a farm accident, he spent 31 years working at Goodyear's Uranium Enrichment Plant. After retiring, he became a manager of a textbook store at Shawnee State University.[68]

Commander Page Knight, the second commanding officer for VB-110, after leaving FAW-7 became Commander of Air Group 151 flying F4U Corsair fighters. He later served with CINCLANT and SACLANT as Assistant Chief of Staff for Plans and Navy Liaison Officer with the Army at Fort Monroe before retiring as a Captain in 1965.[69]

Gene S. McIntyre spent his youth in Memphis and Millington, Tennessee. After graduating from Christian Brothers College in 1936, he held several Jobs including one at a TNT Plant. In 1941, McIntyre joined the Royal Canadian Air Force (R.C.A.F.) and trained as a pilot at Regina, Saskatchewan. Six weeks before graduating from flight school, Pearl Harbor was attacked and he resigned from the R.C.A.F. to join the U.S. Navy. After his tour with VB-103 ended in June 1944, he served at Norfolk where he met his future wife, Zola Maxine Harry. After being released from Navy in October 1945, he briefly worked for the U.S. Civil Service before becoming a distributor for the Philco, Whirlpool, and Motorola companies. Before retiring and moving to San Antonio, Texas, he owned a retail TV and furniture business in Houston. After retiring, he decided to find his VB-103 shipmates and found enough to hold reunion. In 1998, after realizing the squadron's reunion conflicted with the FAW-7 reunion, he teamed up with Mel Stokes and FAW-7 reunions are held annually.[70]

One of the Patrol Plane Commanders briefly mentioned in the book was Lieutenant Bruce Morgan of VB-103. After the war, he went on to become a Hollywood stuntman appearing in hundreds of westerns from the late 1940s to the early 1960s. While working on the movie, *How the West Was Won* in 1962, Morgan was injured requiring the amputation of the left leg. Not satisfied with his prosthesis, Morgan invented a lightweight and less expensive prosthesis. After his first wife Helen died in 1955, he later married the actress Yvonne DeCarlo, which lasted 20 years. He died on 4 March 1999.[71]

Lieutenant Charles P. Muckenthaler and his crew 16 became the first in VB-103 to complete the required 30 missions and departed England on 28 March 1944. For Muckenthaler, World War

The Trevelque hotel at St. Eval as it looked in 2002 housed U.S. Navy officers who were stationed at the nearby airfield (Courtesy of Mike Jarrett).

Mike Jarrett, Dunkeswell Historian (Courtesy of Mike Jarrett).

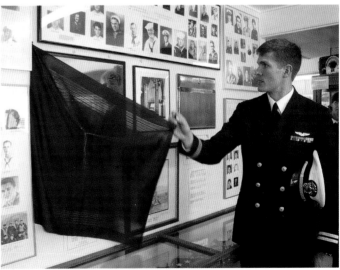

A composite photo done by Mike Jarrett showing him and Bernard Stevens (Courtesy of Mike Jarrett).

II wasn't over. He retrained as a fighter pilot, served aboard the U.S.S. *Lexington*, participated in the invasion of Okinawa, raids on mainland Japan, and flew Combat Air Patrol (CAP) over the Japanese surrender ceremony aboard the U.S.S. *Missouri* in Tokyo Bay. On his thoughts about World War II, "It was a piss poor war, but it was better than nothing." He retired from the Navy with the rank of Captain.

Commander Francis E. Nuessle, the first commanding officer of VB-105 rose to the rank of Captain and went on to command the aircraft carrier U.S.S. *Midway* during the late 1950s.

Commander Jame R. Reedy's (first commanding officer of VB-110) post-FAW-7 military career consisted of being on the NATO staff in Paris, Commander Carrier Division 20, U.S. Antarctic Sup-

port Force, Commander Task Force 77, Carrier Division 5, and a staff officer with Chief of Naval Operations. In 1963, he opened the first U.S. Mail run from Capes Town, South Pole to Antarctica with the story appearing in a 1964 issue of National Geographic. He retired as a Rear Admiral in 1968 and died in San Antonio, Texas on 8 January 1999.

Lieutenant Charles F. "Whiskey" after the war founded Willis Air Service with $13,000, which grew into an international air freight service. He then founded Teterboro School of Aeronautics, two airport fuel and service businesses, Aircraft Services International, and the Willis-Rose Corporation. Mr. Willis was co-founder of Citizens for Eisenhower that popularized the "I Like Ike," slogan and helped persuade Eisenhower to run for President in 1952. During Presi-

The late Bernard Stevens, Dunkeswell Historian, in 2000 (Courtesy of Mike Jarrett).

Lt. Josh Dittmar (U.S.N.), unveiling the plaque for Bernard Stevens at the Dunkeswell Memorial Museum on Memorial Day 2001 (Courtesy of Dunkeswell Memorial Museum).

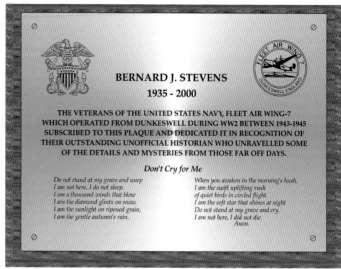

This plaque was donated by the veterans of Fleet Air Wing-7 in honor of their very high esteem for Bernard Stevens (Courtesy of Dunkeswell Memorial Museum).

"Many returned home, some stayed forever, none will be forgotten" (Courtesy of Dunkeswell Memorial Museum).

dent Eisenhower's Administration, Willis served as a special White House assistant and chairman of the United States Committee for the United Nations. In 1957, he became head of Alaska Airlines. Other accomplishments include helping develop pilot training for Japan Airlines and guiding the creation of Korean Airlines. His four marriages ended in divorce but produced two daughters and three sons. He died of lung cancer in Washington D.C. at the age of 74 in March 1993.[72]

Lieutenant Owen D. Windall joined United Air Lines in 1946 and worked for them until furloughed in 1948. Afterward, he flew Douglas DC-4's and Curtis C-46's for Coastal and Flying Tiger Air Lines until he was recalled by United in 1950 with whom he remained with until his retirement.[73]

Bernard Stevens, the young boy who watched the PB4Y-1s take of and, as an adult, helped keep the memory of Fleet Air Wing Seven Liberator squadrons alive, was born on 19 November 1935.

After his mother died in 1947, he went to live with his uncle where he left school and became a baker. He joined the R.A.F. National Service and served for three years until health problems caused his discharge. He resumed baking for 22 years until his death in 2000.[74]

Mike Jarrett after spending his youth in Dunkeswell worked as a Technical Manager for the BBC in London from 1955 to 1989. When Mike retired, he returned to his 'roots' and settled about six miles from the Dunkeswell airfield. When he decided to visit the airfield one last time, Mike heard there was a group of people who were thinking of starting a museum dedicated to all those who lost their lives. The volunteers wanted to provide a viewing platform for those younger members of the public who know little or nothing of the historic significance of the airfield. He volunteered to join the group and, several months later, there was an inaugural meeting at the museum which, by that time, had sought and gained charitable status.[75]

Gallery:
Color Profiles and Assorted Photos

The Hedron 7 logo (Courtesy of Dunkeswell Memorial Museum).

The VB/VPB-103 logo was produced by commercial artist Leon Schlessenger, and approved by the Chief of Naval Operations on 3 February 1945. It features the rabbit Bugs Bunny riding a bomb while eating a carrot. The bomb represents the designation of the squadron while the rabbit represents the speed of the PB4Y-1 (Information from the Dictionary of American Aviation Squadrons, Vol. 2. Photograph Courtesy of Dunkeswell Memorial Museum).

VB-105

VB-110

The VB/VPB-105 logo dates back to 1931 and features a patrolman chasing after an unseen wrongdoer (Information from the Dictionary of American Aviation Squadrons, Vol. 2. Courtesy of Dunkeswell Memorial Museum).

The VB/VPB-110 logo was approved by the Chief of Naval Operations on 3 February 1945 and features a fox holding a pair of binoculars in his left paw and a bomb in his right paw while straddling a .50-caliber machine gun. The binoculars were the primary device for spotting German U-boats while the machine gun and the bomb were the PB4Y-1's primary weapons (Information from the Dictionary of American Aviation Squadrons, Vol. 2. Courtesy of Dunkeswell Memorial Museum).

VB/VPB-114 logo was initially approved by the Chief of Naval Operations on 23 May 1943. (Information from the Dictionary of American Aviation Squadrons, Vol. 2. Courtesy of Dunkeswell Memorial Museum).

An experimental color photo of civilian workers taken at Dunkeswell in 1944 (Courtesy of Dunkeswell Memorial Museum).

The bombed coast of France taken by George Koshiol of VB-110 sometime after D-Day (Courtesy of George Koshiol via Dunkeswell Memorial Museum).

Carper standing at the ready at the waist position behind a .50-caliber machinegun (Courtesy of George Koshiol via Dunkeswell Memorial Museum).

A hoist being used to remove an engine from "L" B-11 of VB-110 (Courtesy of George Koshiol via Dunkeswell Memorial Museum).

A local farm house near the air field (Courtesy of George Koshiol via Dunkeswell Memorial Museum).

L. Francisco of VB-110 piloting his PB4Y-1 during a patrol over the Bay of Biscay (Courtesy of George Koshiol via Dunkeswell Memorial Museum).

A British Wellington bomber taken by George Koshiol of VB-110 (Courtesy of George Koshiol via Dunkeswell Memorial Museum).

Left: George Koshiol of VB-110 with a pet monkey (Courtesy of George Koshiol via Dunkeswell Memorial Museum).

Omaha Beach after D-Day (Courtesy of George Koshiol via Dunkeswell Memorial Museum).

Point Du Hoc after D-Day (Courtesy of George Koshiol via Dunkeswell Memorial Museum).

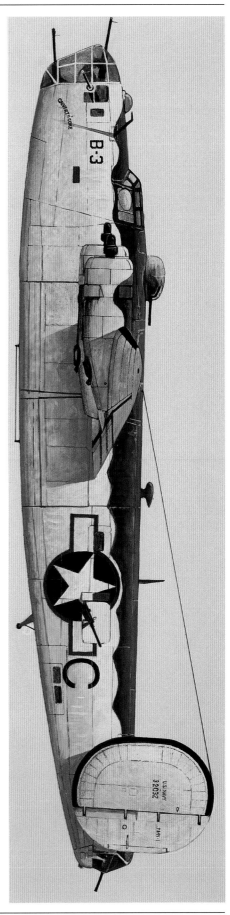

Bureau Number 32032 (ex USAAF 42-40429) B-3 "C" *Calvert & Coke* **of VB-103, 1943**
Calvert & Coke **was an early D-model Liberator with standard coloring of non-specular sea blue and non-specular insignia white. This aircraft was lost in action along with Lt. Ralph Brownell and his crew on 12 November 1943 while attacking and sinking U-508.**

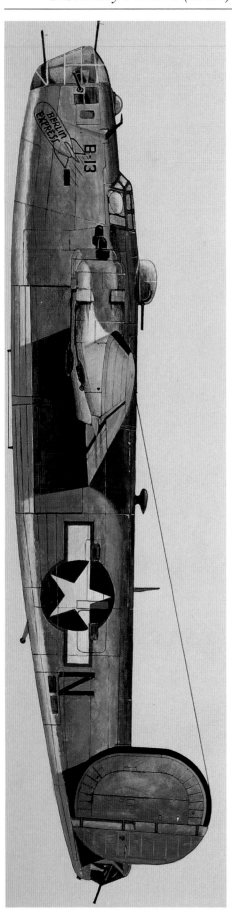

Bureau Number 32014 (ex USAAF 42-40271) B-13 "N" *Berlin Express* **of VB-103, 1943 FAW-7 Navy Liberators appeared to have went through a variety of camouflage schemes during World War II.** *Berlin Express*, **piloted by Lt. Chet Rief and Bruce Higgenbothem, appears to have sported a tri-color camouflage scheme. This aircraft crashed on 3 December 1943 killing another crew.**

Bureau Number 32035 (ex USAAF 42-40435) B-5 "E" *Muck's Mauler* **of VB-103/VPB-113, 1943-1944**
Lt. Charles "Muck" Muckenthaler commanded this D-model PB4Y-1 with non-specular sea blue and non-specular white coloring. During VB-103's deployment to Argentia, New-foundland, the original coloration for *Muck's Mauler* **may have been olive drab uppers and gull gray lower surfaces. This aircraft was lost on 28 December 1944 while being ferried back to the U.S. by VPB-113, killing all 13 men aboard.**

Bureau Number 90474 B-12 "M" *Piccadilly Pam* **of VB/VPB-103, 1944-45.**
Piccadilly Pam **was an M-model Liberator that sported an ERCO bow turret and a rear mounted astrodome. ERCO-equipped Liberators began arriving in Great Britain in early 1944. Note the APS-15 search radar that replaced the Sperry belly turret. This aircraft came to an inglorious end when she was scrapped at Stillwater, Oklahoma after World War II.**

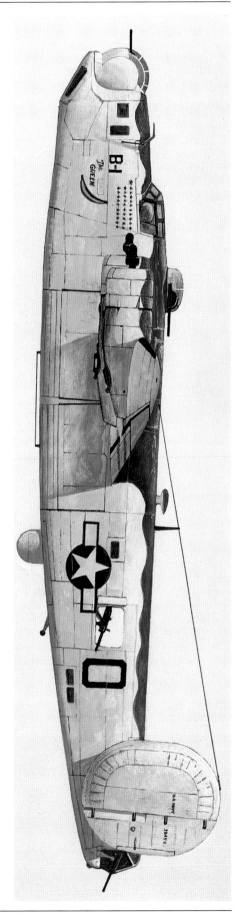

Bureau Number 63944 B-1 "O" *The Green Banana* **of VB/VPB-105, 1944-45.**
The Green Banana **was a D-model PB4Y-1 and flown by Crew 7B of VB/VPB-105. It was being ferried back to the United States by another crew on 14 January 1945 when it crashed into a mountain in French Morocco killing all on board.**

B-2 "P" *The Solid Character* **of VB-105, 1944-45**
The plane captain of *The Solid Character*, **Karl Bertram, was a jazz pianist from Cincinnati, Ohio. The aircraft was named on his honor and Donald McDonald painted a "zoot suited jive" character on the side of the plane. The thought process is from the swing and jitterbug slang of the late 30s and early 40s. Note the 50 mission markings and one aerial kill painted below the cockpit.**

Bureau Number 32283 (ex USAAF 42-110126) B-6 "T" of VB-105, 1944-45.
A few J-model Navy Liberators retained the Emerson nose turret and a "high hat" upper turret. Note the sea-blue replacement rudders. This aircraft was flown back to the United States after the war.

Bureau Number 63923 B-1 "A" of VB-110, 1944
This is a D-model Liberator has an ERCO bow turret, rear-mounted astrodome, and APS-15 radar. It appears to have survived the war and was flown back to the United States.

Bureau Number 38885 No. 85 "E" of VPB-112, Upottery Field 1945
In January 1945, VPB-112 was transferred from French Morocco to Upottery Field, England. This J-model Liberator has the standard coloring of non-specular sea blue uppers and non-specular insignia white lowers. This aircraft was flown to Clinton, Oklahoma in July 1945 and scrapped.

Bureau Number 32192 (ex USAAF 42-73170) No. 231 "J" of VB-114, 1944-1945
Leigh Light-equipped Navy Liberators of Navy Bombing Squadron VB/VPB-114 were
sent to England in June 1944 and operated from Dunkeswell until February 1945. This is
a D-model PB4Y-1 and was commanded by Lt. Oren W. Clark.

RAF Serial Number FL-933 GR. III Liberator of No. 120 Squadron, Coastal Command, Northern Ireland 1942-1943,
Before and during FAW-7's time in Great Britain, RAF Coastal Command deployed a significant number of B-24s against U-boats. The Royal Air Force was provided 366 B-24D Liberators and were fitted with the four-machine gun Boulton Paul tail turret. FL-933 has an early antennae farm on the fuselage and under the wing. Note the absence of the top turret on the GR. III and VI (below). FL-933 was sold as scrap in 1947.

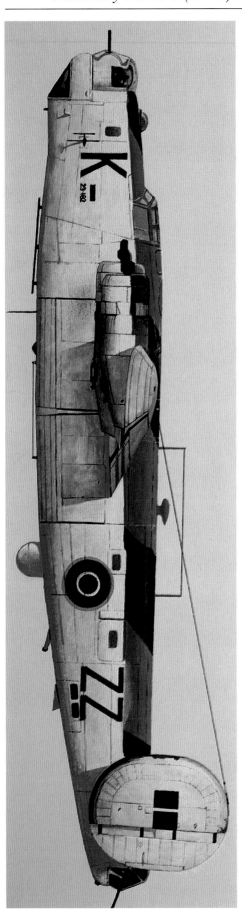

GR. VI of No. 220 Squadron, Coastal Command, Lagens, Azores 1944-45
The British version of the B-24J, this GR. VI has the APS-15 radar and Consolidated nose and tail turrets. It seems unlikely that British Liberators were fitted with the ERCO bow turret.

Glossary:
World War II U.S. Navy Terminology

AB:	Aerial Bombardier usually an enlisted man.
AP:	An enlisted Aviation Pilot and is equivalent to sergeant in the R.A.F.
BuAer:	Bureau of Aeronautics.
CAP:	Chief Aviation Pilot.
COMAIRLANT:	Commander Airforce Atlantic Fleet.
FAW:	Fleet Air Wing.
PATSU:	Patrol Aircraft Service Unit. Responsible for minor maintenance duties and engine checks.
PPC:	Patrol Plane Commander.
SAU:	Special Air Unit.
VB:	Bombing Squadron.
VP:	Patrol Squadron.
VPB:	Patrol Bombing Squadron. VB became VPB on 1 October 1944.

Navy Rank Structure for Commissioned Officers

U.S. Navy	**U.S. Army Air Force**
Ensign (Ens.)	Second Lieutenant
Lieutenant (jg)	First Lieutenant
Lieutenant (Lt.)	Captain
Lieutenant Commander (Lt. Cmdr.)	Major
Commander (Cmdr.)	Lieutenant Colonel
Captain (Capt.)	Full Colonel
Commodore	Special rank between Captain and Admiral with no Air Force equivalent.
Rear Admiral (lower half)	Brigadier General
Rear Admiral (upper half)	Major General
Vice Admiral	Lieutenant General
Admiral	General
Fleet Admiral	Five Star General

World War II Enlisted Navy Rating and Rate

Rating: The occupational specialty as indicated by a symbol above the chevrons (most enlisted crewmembers on PB4Y-1 aircraft were utilized as aerial gunners).

Rate: Pay grade indicated by the number of chevrons.

Ratings

Aviation Machinist Mate (AMM)	maintains all aspects of aircraft maintenance
Aviation Ordnanceman (AOM)	maintains all guns, turrets, and bombs
Aviation Radioman (ARM)	maintains and operates all radio and radar equipment
Aviation Radio Technician (ART)	maintains all radio equipment
Aviation Machinist Mate-Aviation Flight Engineer (AMMF)	
Seaman First Class (S1c)	
Seaman Second Class (S2c)	
Chief Petty Officer Ratings	
Aviation Chief Machinists Mate (ACMM)	
Aviation Chief Radioman (ACRM)	
Aviation Chief Ordnanceman (ACOM)	

Rates

1c:	1st Class
2c:	2nd Class
3c:	3rd Class

German Rank System

German	U.S. Army Airforce	U.S. Navy
Leutnant	Second Lieutenant	Ensign
Feldwebel	Flight Sergeant	
Kapitänleutnant	Major	Lieutenant Commander
Oberleutnant	First Lieutenant	Lieutenant (jg)
Oberleutnant zur See	Captain	Lieutenant
Unteroffizier		Sergeant

Appendix A:
Organizational Structure of FAW-7
October 1943-May 1945
(Source: FAW-7 Report)

FAW-7 Command Structure European Theater October 1943
Operating under Task Force 24
FAW-7 Command Headquarters (Commodore W. H. Hamilton)
HEDRON-7 (Lieutenant Commander J. T. Moynahan)
Patrol Aircraft Service Units (PATSU)
Patrol Air Group 1
Dunkeswell Air Group (Commander William T. Easton)
Group Commander and staff
VB-103 (Commander William Von Bracht)
VB-105 (Commander Francis E. Nuessle)
Headquarters Base Unit
PATSU-103
PATSU-105
St. David's Group (Commander E.O. Wagner)
Group Commander and staff
VB-110 (Lieutenant Commander James Reedy)
VB-111 (Commander M.H. Tuttle)
Headquarters Squadron Station Service
PATSU-110
PATSU-111
Pembroke Dock Group
VP-63
PATSU-63
355 officers
1,877 enlisted

FAW-7 Command Structure European Theater April 1944
FAW-7 Command Headquarters (Commodore William H. Hamilton)
HEDRON-7 (Commander J. T. Moynahan)
Base Unit
PATSU
Patrol Air Group 1
U.S. Navy Air Facility Dunkeswell (Commander Thomas Durfee)
VB-103 (Commander William Von Bracht)
PATSU 103
VB-105 (Lieutenant Commander Donald F. Gay)
PATSU 105
VB-110 (Lieutenant Commander James R. Reedy)
PATSU 110
361 officers
2,081 enlisted

FAW-7 Command Structure European Theater 1 January 1945
FAW-7 (Commodore William H. Hamilton)
HEDRON-7 (Commander J. T. Moynahan)
U.S. Navy Air Facility Dunkeswell (Commander George C. Miller)
Patrol Air Group 1 (Commander J. R. Reedy)
VPB-103 (Commander W. J. Bettens)
VPB-107 (Lieutenant Commander W.F. Brewer,)
VPB-105 (Lieutenant Commander L. E. Harmon)
VPB-110 (Commander Page Knight)
VPB-112 (Commander Aram Y. Parunak)
VPB-114 Detachment (Commander C. F. Skuzinski)
Patrol Air Group 2 at Upottery (Commander James E. Johnson)
VP-63 Detachment (Lieutenant Commander Carl A. Benscotter)

FAW-7 Command Structure European Theater 1 May 1945
12th Fleet, Task Force 121
Commander-in-Chief 12th Fleet (Admiral Harold R. Stark)
Task Group 121.1 FAW-7,
Command Headquarters (Rear Admiral Andrew C. McFall)
Task Group 121.6 HEDRON-7 (Lieutenant Commander
    Roger D. Hutchins)
Task Group 121.2 Patrol Air Group 1 (Commander
    Robert S. Camera)
VPB-103 (Lieutenant Commander Warren J. Bettens)
VPB-105 (Lieutenant Commander Leonard E. Harmon)
VPB-110 (Lieutenant Commander Duncan A. Campbell)
VP-63 Detachment (Lieutenant Commander Carl A. Benscotter)
PATSU 7-A
PATSU 7-B
PATSU 7-C
PATSU 7-E
HEDRON-7 (Lieutenant Commander Roger D. Hutchins)
Task Group 121.3 Patrol Air Group 2 at Naval Satellite Facility,
Upottery (Commander James E. Johnson)
VP-63 Detachment
VPB-107 (Lieutenant Commander William F. Brewer)
VPB-112 (Commander John B. Wayne)
PATSU 7-F
PATSU 7-G
Officers=444
Enlisted=2,560

Appendix B:
Commanding Officers of FAW-7
and Individual Squadrons
May 1943-May 1945

FAW-7
Commodore William H. Hamilton to 31 March 1945
Rear Admiral Andrew C. McFall from 31 March 1945

Commanding Officers Dunkeswell Naval Facility
Commander Thomas Durfee to 30 June 1944
Lieutenant Commander Henry W. King from 30 June-4 July 1944
Commander George C. Miller from 4 July 1944

Air Group 1
Commander James R. Reedy to 23 January 1945
Commander Robert S. Camera from 23 January 1945

Air Group 2
Commander James E. Johnson from 20 January 1945

HEDRON-7
Commander James T. Moynahan to 14 April 1945
Lieutenant Commander Roger D. Hutchins from 14 April 1945

Squadron Commanders

VB/VPB-103
Lieutenant Commander William T. Easton from 15 March to 20 August 1943
Lieutenant Commander William G. Von Bracht from 20 August 1943 to 8 July 1944
Lieutenant Commander Warren J. Bettens from 8 July 1944 to 24 June 1945

VB/VPB-105
Commander Francis E. Nuessle from 1 January 1942 to 1 January 1944
Lieutenant Commander Donald F. Gay from 1 January to 1 September 1944
Lieutenant Commander Leonard E. Harmon from 1 October 1944 to 17 May 1945
Lieutenant Commander John K. Sloatman Jr., from 17 May to 27 to June 1945

VB/VPB-107
(Upottery Deployment)
Lieutenant Commander William F. Brewer from 25 January 1945

VB/VPB-110
Lieutenant Commander James R. Reedy 18 July 1943 to 28 April 1944
Lieutenant Commander Page Knight 28 April to 27 December 1944
Commander George C. Miller 27 December 1944 to 12 January 1945
Lieutenant Commander Duncan A. Campbell 12 January to 1 September 1945

VB/VPB-112
(Upottery Deployment)
Commander Aram Y. Parunak to 4 April 1945
Lieutenant Commander John B. Wayne from 4 April 1945

Appendix C:
Personnel Losses by All Causes

VB-103

Losses in Newfoundland

24 June 1943

Crew failed to return from operational mission

Name	Rank
Herbert Kearsley Reese Jr.	Lieutenant
Willis Albert Schafer	Ensign
Walter Erwin Hedtke	AP1c
Raymond Rainsfield Ross Jr.	AOM1c
Norman Edward Rendall III	ARM1c
Richard Franklin Simpson	AMM2c
Melville Lucius Dickerson	ART2c
Robert Thomas Douglas	AOM2c
Harold Ferman Valenseula	AMM3c
Henry Edward Whittlake	ARM3c

7 August 1943

Crashed at sea during a training mission

Name	Rank
Walter Bruce Henry	Lieutenant (jg)
James George Hamilton	Ensign
Rex Irwin Beach	Ensign
Norman Ford Dennis	ARM3c
Winford Fred McVey	AMM3c
Frank Charles Sorenson	ARM3c
Charles Junior Branche	AOM3c
Orion Dewey Snow	AOM3c
William Lewis Denney	AOM3c
Raymond Russell Gardner	ARM2c
Francis Robert Grest	ARM2c

VB/VPB-103

Losses in England

2 September 1943

Failed to return from an operational mission

Name	Rank
Keith Wilbur Wickstrom	Lieutenant
Carlyle Knoeer Martin	Ensign
Roy Leslie Perry	AP1c
Willard Bruce Wadsworth	ARM2c
Nels Mose LaRue	AMM1c
Morris Steinberg	ARM3c
Richard John Olsen	AOM2c
Wallace Berk Marshburn	AMM3c
Jack Nathan Rubin	S2c

November 12 1943

Shot down while attacking U-boat

Name	Rank
Ralph Bliss Brownell	Lieutenant (jg)
Daniel Anthony Schneider	Ensign
Kendall Ridgeway Poole	CAP
William English	AMM1c
George Benjamin Simpson Jr.	AMM2c
Bobbie Russell Holladay	ARM1c
Walter Nelson Meroney	AMM3c
Charles Kenneth McClung	AOM2c
Leland Eitel	AOM2c
Walter Clarence Rogers Jr.	S1c

3 December 1943

Crashed on training flight

Name	Rank
Tony Anthony Lucas	Lieutenant
James Herbert Alexander Jr.	Lieutenant (jg)
Donald Barrett Shea	Ensign
Francis James Buckley	Ensign
Theodore Lemoine Ray	AMM1c
Wilse Adolph Bean	ARM2c
William H. Davidson	AOM1c (AB)
James Woodrow Laubinger	AOM2c
Eldred Aliysious Shubert	AMM3c
Richard James O'Leary	AMM2c

30 January 1944
Killed on the ground at RAF Station, Talbenny, United Kingdom

Name	Rank
Chadwick Buford Jarrett	ARM3c
George Washington Josey Jr.	ARM3c

14 February 1944
Killed when plane ditched at sea after being attacked by JU-88s

Name	Rank
Bennie Faubion	AOM2c
Robert Charles Erdman	ARM2c
Thomas Edwin Ryan	ARM2c

20 March 1944
Crashed at sea during operational mission

Name	Rank
Jack Cooper Kessel	Lieutenant (jg)
Robert Emmet Holloran	Ensign
Donald Harrison Ballard	Ensign
Orville James Parks	AMM1c
Charles Burvel Newcombe	ARM1c
Orville Melvin Collingwood	ARM2c
Arthur Edward Robinson	AOM2c (AB)
Albert Leo McKinney Jr.	AMM3c
Robert Allen Sayers	AMM2c
James Stephen Curley	AOM2c
Cecil Lewis Meekins	AOM3c
Edward Franklin Garloff Jr.	ARM3c

VB-105

10 September 1943
Crashed at sea near Cornwall during training flight

Name	Rank
George W. Brown	Lieutenant (jg)
Jack C. Siens	Lieutenant (jg)
Thomas A. Friend	ACRM
James G. Conlon	AMM2c
Lester H. Whiting	AMM2c
Raymond G. Keenan	AMM3c
Jessie G. Smith	AOM1c
Carl E. Griese	ARM3c

22 October 1943
Failed to return from mission over the Bay of Biscay

Name	Rank
Thomas R. Evert	Lieutenant
David W. Emmett	Lieutenant (jg)
James H. O'Hara	Ensign
Edward J. Ellis	Ensign
Kendall L. Dungey	AMM3c
Donald Sweeney	AMM3c
John F. Wagner	ARM2c
James T. Goble	ARM2c
Brown H. Smith	AMM2c
Raymond Haines	AMM2c

23 October 1943
Crashed on take-off at St. Eval

Name	Rank
John C. Hillman	Lieutenant (jg)
Armand E. Trafton	Lieutenant (jg)
Edwin C. Creeger Jr.	Ensign
Clyde E. Rodgers	AMM1c
Morgan T. Charland Jr.	AMM2c
William O. Finch	ARM1c
John C. Mowatt	ARM2c
Lawrence L. Wemette	AMM3c
Ralph H. Cole	AOM3c
Brewton Massey Jr.	AOM3c

26 February 1944
Failed to return from mission over Bay of Biscay

Name	Rank
Raymond L. North	Lieutenant
John E. Goodrich	Lieutenant (jg)
Victor D'Harlingue	Ensign
Harold L. Counts	AMM1c
Walter F. Brown	ARM1c
Frederick J. Malounek	AMM2c
Lee R. Merritt	AOM3c
John R. Van Benschoten	AMM2c
William W. Pendleton	AMM3c
Walter Pawlyk	ARM3c

3 January 1945
Crashed into Beacon Hill while attempting
to land at RAF Base, Exeter

Name	Rank
George Egidio Pantano	Lieutenant
Martin Wayne Garber	Ensign
Andy Elmer Simmons	AMM3c
George Andrew Matta	AMM3c
Walter Joseph Antonik	AOM1c
Andrew Scott Pelath	S1c (ARM)

VB-110

8 November 1943
Shot down by enemy aircraft

Name	Rank
W. E. Grumbles	Lieutenant
A.F. Wentworth	Ensign

J.T. Drinkwater	Ensign
James E. Dennis	AMM2c
Winfred B. Hay	AMM3c
Charles J. Kavanagh	ARM3c
James H. Cole	AOM3c
Gerald H. Johnston	AMM2c
Carl F. Kelly	S1c

28 December 1943
Crashed near Okehampton, England while returning from operational mission

Name	Rank
W.W. Parish	Lieutenant
D.M. Lyons	Ensign
R.W. Lovelace	Ensign
A.J. Stork	AMM2c
J.E. Schaffer	AMM2c
L.M. Davenport	ARM2c
J.F. Benson	ARM3c
A.J. Roddy Jr.	AOM3c
G.A. Reynard	AMM3c
D.E. Nash	AMM3c

26 February 1944
Crashed into Great Skellig Rock while returning from operational mission

Name	Rank
J.L. Williams	Lieutenant
C.W. Quigle	Lieutenant(jg)
K.L. Bowman	Ensign
E.G. Willis Jr.	ACMM(AA)
G.E. Davison	AMM2c
J.A. Huffman Jr.	ARM2c
H.C. Crow	ARM3c
J.E. McLaughlin	AOM3c
E.W. Libby	AMM3c
J.T. Flener	S2c
M.J. Olsen	S2c

12 March 1944
Disappeared near Cherbourg on operational mission

Name	Rank
W.H. Ryan	Lieutenant(jg)
J.J. Shea	Ensign
W. Sharkey	Ensign
C.E. Burger	AMM1c
W.H. Schultz	AMM3c
T.J Howard	ARM2c
W.E. Greenfield	ARM3c
M.R. Jones	AOM3c
H.B. Combs	AMM3c
M.F. Regan	AMM3c

31 March 1944
Shot down by enemy fighters

Name	Rank
H. Barton	Lieutenant
R.J. Schuetz	Lieutenant (jg)
P.W. Bash	Ensign
W.J. Ketchen	ACMM(AA)
W.F. Smith	AMM3c
R.P. Krebs	AMM2c
D.V.J. Timberman	ARM2c
A.P. Oliver	ARM3c
D.C. Gamble	AOM2c
E.H. McLean	ARM3c
R.W. Mellette	AOM2c,

B-11L, 31 March 1944

O.H. Moore	Lieutenant(jg)
G.A. Rapp	Lieutenant (jg)
R.M. Kreuger	Ensign
S.R. Clayton	AMM1c
W.A. Doerich	AMM2c
W.N. Swanson	ARM1c
P.I. Jordan	ARM2c
J.R. Stewart	AOM2c
H.O. Prattar	AMM2c
G.P. Enfieger	S2c

24 August 1944

Crashed near Breckon, South Wales while conducting training flight

Name	Rank
John Glennon Byrnes	Lieutenant (jg)
John Neill Hobson Jr.	Lieutenant (jg)
Andrew Manelski	Ensign
Hyman Price Holt Jr.	AMM1c
Franklin Richard Shipe	ARM2c
Donald Franklin Kiester	AMM3c

VB-111

13 October 1943

Killed when ferrying PB4Y-1 from Norfolk to UK

Name	Rank
Dolive Durant	Lieutenant
Richard Egles	Ensign
Bobbie L. Kennedy	Ensign
K.E. Monsees	AMM2c
D.N. Staver	AMM2c
R.W. Nally	ARM2c
A.W. Nestark	ARM3c
T.F. Chilcote	AOM2c
W.E. Walsh	S1c
J.C. Strong	AMM2c
C.F. Freas	ARM3c
W.G. McNeill	AOM2c

Note: The loss of this aircrew was added to FAW-7 statistics, as the destination for the aircraft and crew was Dunkeswell.

FAW-7

12 August 1944

Lost when BQ-8 drone exploded in mid-air

Name	Rank
Joe P. Kennedy Jr.	Lieutenant (Special Air Unit)
Willford J. Willy	Lieutenant (Special Air Unit)

15 September 1944

Ditched fuel exhaustion six miles off Irish Coast during ferry flight from Norfolk to Dunkeswell

Name	Rank
Carl Grey Snavely Jr.	Ensign
Phillip A. Mills	Ensign
Vernon H. Peterson	AMM3c
Joseph G. Fleucher	ARM2c
Nathan Beckwith	S1c

14 January 1945

Crashed on ferry flight to Igoudour, French Morocco

Name	Rank
Ralph D. Spalding Jr.	Lieutenant
Milton H. Thuna	Lieutenant (jg)
Milo J. Jones	Ensign
Norman H. Lowrey	AMMF2c
Frank A. Lutz	AMMF3c
Fred W. Rife	ARM1c
Edwin M. Lignar	ARM3c
James T. Hagedorn	AOM2c
Milford D. Merritt	AMM2c
William E. Burns	AOMT3c
Robert W. Baker	AOM3c (passenger)

Total Personnel Losses

Squadron	Number Killed
VB/VPB-103	63
VB/VPB-105	44
VB/VPB-110	67
VB/VPB-111	12
FAW-7	18
Total Losses	204

Note: 21 men where lost while VB-103 was based at Argentia, Newfoundland. FAW-7 lost 17 men while ferrying PB4Y-1s and does not include other losses suffered by VB/VPB-113.

Appendix D:
U-boat Contacts and Kills Attributed
to FAW-7 PB4Y-1 Liberators

Possible radar, sonobouy contacts, or oil slicks are not included. This does not include an attack made by VB-103 while based at Argentia, Newfoundland. Data compiled with the assistance of Mike Jarrett.

Date	Pilot/Squadron	Remarks
24/10/43	Lt. North/VB-105	Possible damage
10/11/43	Lt. Wright/VB-103	U966 with Liberator "D" 311 Squadron RAF
10/11/43	Lt. Harmon/VB-105	U966
10/11/43	Lt. Parish/VB-110	U966
12-11-43	Lt. Brownell/VB-103	U508
28-1-44	Lt. Enloe/VB-103	U271 sunk
29/1/44	Lt. Rudd/VB-110	
13/2/44	Lt. Steale/VB-103	
2/3/44	Lt. Ellis/VB-103	
30/4/44	Lt. Trum/VB-103	Possible damage
16/5/44	Lt. (jg) Higginbotham/VB-103	
8/6/44	Lt. Koskinen/VB-105	Possible slight damage
13/6/44	Lt. Johnson/VB-110	
13/6/44	Lt. Cdr. Munson/VB-110	
18/6/44	Lt. Auslander/VB-105	Possible slight damage to U767
22/6/44	Lt. Foulks/VB-103	Possible damage oil slick 3-4 miles and wreckage
22/6/44	Lt.Spalding/VB-110	
22/6/44	Lt. Windall/VB-103	Possible damage to U971
22/6/44	Lt. Felson/VB-110	
23/6-44	Lt. Hmay/VB-103	Possible slight damage debris
23/6/44	Ens. Sivo/VB-103	
23/6/44	Lt. Duffy/VB-110	
8/7/44	Lt. Cooledge/VB-105	With Sunderlands H&K of 10 Squadron U243 sunk
28/7/44	Lt. Filson/VB-110	Possible damage to U333
8/8/44	Lt. Duffy/VB-110	Possible slight damage
10/8/44	Lt. Seymore/VB-110	Possible slight damage
26/8/44	Lt. Deutsch/VB-103	Disappearing radar contact Sonobuoy indications
17/9/44	Lt. Chamberlain/VB-105	Possible damage
23/2/45	Lt. Ostroski/VPB-103	
27/2/45	Lt. Dennison/VPB-112	Spotted U327 and sunk by 2nd Escort Group
11/3/45	Lt. Field/VPB-103	U681 sunk
26/3/45	Lt. (jg) Papas/VPB-110	
22/4/45	Lt. Hyke/VPB-110	
25/4/45	Lt. Nott/VPB-103	U326 sunk

Appendix E:
FAW-7 PB4Y-1 Operational Sorties
(Source: FAW-7 Official Reports)

1943

Squadron	Aug	Sept	Oct	Nov	Dec
103	38*	49	60	59	57
105		-	52	61	57
110		-	18	70	79

*Sorties from Argentia=36 and 2 from St. Eval

1944

Squadron	Jan	Feb	Mar	Apr	May	June	July	Aug	Sep	Oct	Nov	Dec
103	51	82	107	74	77	156	133	124	116	77	98	103
105	40	83	113	63	74	154	130	126	108	80	97	98
110	53	88	107	63	77	160	131	130	113	72	101	101
114	-	-	-	-	-	4	33	42	35	24	32	22

1945

Squadron	Jan	Feb	Mar	Apr	May
103	75	68	113	108	77
105	80	70	112	107	69
107	-	8	74	70	24
110	78	70	111	108	76
112	-	27	99	93	42
114	12	2	-	-	-

Appendix F:
PB4Y-1 Losses
1 May 1943-1 May 1945

Squadron	Losses
103	14
105	9
107	0 (January-May 1945)
110	11
111	1 (October 1943)
112	0 (January-May 1945)
114	1 (Dunkeswell Detachment June 1944-February 1945)
FAW-7	2
SAU-1	2
Total=	40

Appendix G:
Squadron Disposition of PB4Y-1s
(Sources: Individual Squadron Reports,
FAW-7 Reports, and Individual Flight Logs)

The following is a list of PB4Y-1 Liberators known to have been assigned to FAW-7. The data was compiled with the assistance of Mike Jarrett.

VB/VPB-103

Bureau No.	Name	Remarks
32013 "A" B-1		To U.S. for overhaul 20/12/43
32014 "N" B-13	*Berlin Express*	Later changed to B-2 Loss 3/12/43
32015 "K" B-10	*Tally Ho! The Fox! She Runs!*	To U.S. for overhaul
32017		Loss 4/10/43
32018 B-14		To U.S. for overhaul 3/1/44
32022 "G" B-7	*Impatient Virgin*	Lost in Action. Ditched off Spanish Coast 9/4/43
32023 "O"		To U.S. for overhaul 26/8/44
32027		To U.S. for overhaul 20/12/43
32028 B-15	*Kee Bird*	Changed to B-2. To U.S. for overhaul 3/1/44
32029 B-2		
32030		Ex VB-111 and transferred to VB-105. Scrapped at Stillwater, Oklahoma
32032 "C" B-3	*Calvert & Coke*	Shot down attacking U-508 12/11/43 10 killed
32033 "D" B-4		Lost in Action 2/9/43 9 killed
32035 "E" B-5	*Muck's Mauler*	Crashed on ferry flight to U.S. 13 killed
32036	*Box Car*	To U.S. for overhaul
32037 B-11	*Wramblin Wreck*	Crashed into Placentia Bay 11 killed 7/8/43
32039 "B" B-6	*Bozo*	Crash landing St. Eval 23/9/43
32040 "H" B-8	*Lady Ritz*	Crash landing at Broadclyst 2/12/43
32046 B-9	*Elmundo the Great?*	Lost on patrol in North Atlantic 24/6/43 10 killed
32191 "C"		
32179 "A"	*Zombie*	Became B-11 "L" obsolete 21/5/45
32183 "B"		Lack of fuel to reach diversion base Gibraltar 29/12/43
32184 "B"		Transferred to VPB-107
32188 "J"		Transferred to Port Lyautey 2/4/45
32191 "C"	*Worry Bird*	Ditched off NW of Cornwall 14/2/44
32200 "H" B-8		Crash landing from mission 9/12/44
32201		Destroyed in ground collision 27/5/44
32203 "M"		Transferred to VPB-107
32207 "K"		Transferred to VPB-107
32209 "L"		Lost near Cherbourg 20/3/44
32210		Assigned to VB-110
32211 "E"		
32212 "C"		Obsolete Transferred to Port Lyautey 10/3/45
32023 "O"		Ex VB-111
32281 "N"		Crashed on take off 24/11/44

32289		Transferred from VPB-105
32290 "A"		
32294 "N"		Ex VPB-105 "C." Assigned to VB-103
32296 "G"		
38748 "P"		To Clinton, Oklahoma 7/45
38784 "O"		Crash landing non operational flight 27/12/44
38810		To Clinton, Oklahoma 7/45
38850		To Clinton, Oklahoma 7/45
38970		To VPB-114 Azores 29/5/45
63957 "D"		To U.S. for overhaul 15/10/44
63958 "F"		To U.S. for overhaul 24/10/44
65314		To VPB-114 Azores 29/5/45
65393		To VPB-114 Azores29/5/45
65394		To VPB-114 Azores29/5/45
65395		
90132 "K"		To VPB-114 Azores 29/5/45
90135		To VPB-114 Azores 30/5/45
90472		
90474 "M" B-12	*Piccadily Pam*	To VPB-114 Azores 29/5/45 Scrapped at Stillwater, Oklahoma

VB/VPB-105

Bureau No.	Name	Remarks
32026		
32038		Ex VB-111 loss 3/17/44
32041		Scrapped Stillwater, Oklahoma
32042		
32199 "P"		To U.S. for overhaul 2/2/45
32236		
32038 "T"		Ex VB-111 Crash landing Talbenny, Wales 17/3/44
32283 "T"		Transferred to VPB-110
32289 "B"		Transferred to VPB-103
32294 "C"		To VPB-103. Broken up at Dunkeswell 6/45
32295 "A"		Broken up at Dunkeswell 6/45
38751 "R"	*Six's Avenger*	To Oklahoma, Clinton 7/45
38785 "S"		To Clinton, Oklahoma 7/45
38784		Crashed on landing 27/12/44
38786		To Clinton, Oklahoma 7/45
38798 "Z"		Ran off the runway on take off 12/11/44
38811 "Q"		Crashed on landing 29/3/45
38839		To Clinton, Oklahoma 7/45
38864 "T"		To Clinton, Oklahoma 7/45
38912		To Clinton, Oklahoma 7/45
38928 "X"		To Clinton, Oklahoma 7/45
38929		To Clinton, Oklahoma 7/45
38930		To Clinton, Oklahoma 7/45
38931 "O"		To Clinton, Oklahoma 7/45
38938		
38947		Crashed into Beacon Hill while attempting to land at Exeter 3/1/45 6 killed
38948 "B"		Caught fire while being fueled for ferry flight 18/7/45
38949		To Clinton, Oklahoma 7/45
39886		
63915 "S" B-5		Crashed on take off for a mission 23/10/43 10 killed
63916 "Q"		To FAW-7 U.S. for overhaul 30/8/44
63917 "P" B-2		Lost in action 22/10/43 10 killed
63918 "W"		To U.S. for overhaul 13/10/44

63924 "U" B-7		To U.S. for overhaul 4/1/45
63925 "O"		Crashed Bude Bay on fighter affiliation 10/9/43 8 killed
63929 "R"		Lost in Action 26/2/44 10 killed
63930 "Z"		To U.S. for overhaul 28/8/44
63933 "T"		To U.S. for overhaul 14/7/44
63935 "V"		To FAW-7 U.S. for overhaul 1/9/44
63936 "Y"		To U.S. for overhaul 7/1/45
63937		To U.S. for overhaul 7/1/45
63938 "X"		To U.S. for overhaul 7/1/45
63944 "O"	*The Green Banana*	Crashed after take off on return flight to U.S. French, Morocco 11/1/45 11 killed
63945		
63954 "S"		Transferred to SAU-1 on 3/9/44 and expended as BQ-8 drone when it exploded near target
90470		To Clinton, Oklahoma 7/45

VPB-107

Bureau No.	Name	Remarks
32184		
32203		
32207		
32211		To U.S. for overhaul 30/3/45
32184		Ex 103 Strike Obsolete 3/30/45 to Port Lyautey
32203		Ex 103 Strike Obsolete 3/30/45 to Port Lyautey
32207		Ex 103 Strike Obsolete 3/30/45 to Port Lyautey
32249		
32250		
32254		
32256		Ex VB-110
32257		
32258		
32211		Ex VPB-103 Strike Obsolete 3/30/45 to Port Lyautey
38866		Ex VPB-112 To Clinton, Oklahoma 7/45
65396		
90195		
90202		
90462		
90473		
32293		

VB/VPB 110

Bureau No.	Name	Remarks
32034		Lost on ferry flight from U.S. to United Kingdom 12 killed
32045 "F"		To U.S. for overhaul 14/7/44
32194 "H"		Ex VB-112 Broken up at Dunkeswell 6/45
32199		Transferred to VPB-105
32210 "B"		Crash landing Chivenor on return from a mission 27/3/44
32236 "N"		Tire blow out on take off for a mission 24/10/44
32237 "B"		Broken up at Dunkeswell 6/45
32256 "L"		Broken up at Dunkeswell 6/45
32282 M B-12		Broken up at Dunkeswell 6/45
32283		Broken up at Dunkeswell 6/45. Assigned from VPB-105
32288 "O" B-14		Broken up at Dunkeswell 6/45
32297 "P"		Broken up at Dunkeswell 6/45
38753 "F"		Crashed on training flight 24/8/44 6 killed
38824		To Clinton, Oklahoma 7/45

38825"J"	To Clinton, Oklahoma 7/45
38826	To Clinton, Oklahoma 7/45
38837	To Clinton, Oklahoma 7/45
38838 "A"	Brake failure on landing 11/3/45
38851	To Clinton, Oklahoma 7/45
38967	To VPB-114 Azores 29/5/45
38968 "N"	To Clinton, Oklahoma 7/45
38969	Searchlight equipped PB4Y-1 transferred VPB-114 Azores 29/5/45
63919"F" B-6	Shot down by enemy fighters 8/11/43 10 killed
63920 "J"	To U.S. for Overhaul
63921 "C" B-3	To U.S. for overhaul 4/12/44
63923 "A"	Transferred to Hedron-7. To U.S. for overhaul
63926 "E" B-5	Crashed returning from mission 28/12/43 10 killed
63928 "K"	Obsolete 10/2/45
63929 to 110	
63932 "D"	To U.S. for overhaul 6/9/44
63934 "B" B-2	Crashed while returning from mission 8/12/43
63937 "G"	To U.S. for overhaul 6/9/44
63939 "H"	Crashed into Great Skelling Rock Ireland 26/2/44 11 killed
63940 "L	Shot down by Ju-88s on patrol 31/3/44 10 killed
63941 "L" B-11	Hedron as utility Aircraft Stricken 12/3/45
63946 "F" B-6	Given incorrect course to base. Lost Near Cherbourg 12/3/44 10 killed
63948 "M" B-12	Shot down by Ju-88s on patrol 31/3/44 11killed
63952 "H/E"	To U.S. 12/12/44

VPB-112

Bureau No.	Name	Remarks
63941		Transferred FAW-7, Strike 3/12/45
63945		Obsolete 21/5/45
63955		Obsolete 21/5/45
32195		Obsolete 21/5/45

Bureau No.		Remarks
38865		To Clinton, Oklahoma 7/45
38885		To Clinton, Oklahoma 7/45
38886		To Clinton, Oklahoma 7/45
38888		To Clinton, Oklahoma 7/45
38909		To Clinton, Oklahoma 7/45
38910		To Clinton, Oklahoma 7/45
38911		To Clinton, Oklahoma 7/45
38937		
38941		
63941		To U.S. for overhaul 18/2/45
63955		

VPB-114 Detachment

Bureau No.	Name	Remarks
32169		Crashed on take off no injuries 5/7/44. Repaired and flown back to U.S. 28/2/45
32192		Fitted with Leigh light
32193		
32197		Fitted with Leigh light
32198		
32202"K"		Fitted with Leigh light
32204		
32205		Fitted with Leigh light
32206		
32335		Fitted with Leigh light
63943"D"		Aircraft transferred from VB-103 assigned to Azores
65314		Scrapped at Stillwater, Oklahoma
65393		Scrapped at Stillwater, Oklahoma
65394		Scrapped at Stillwater, Oklahoma
90132		Scrapped at Stillwater, Oklahoma
90135		Scrapped at Stillwater, Oklahoma

Bibliography

Published Works

Goss, Chris. *Bloody Biscay: The History of Vgruppe/Kampfgeschwader 40*. Crécy Publishing , Ltd., 1997.

Kemp, Paul. *U-boats Destroyed: German Submarine Losses in the World Wars*. Annapolis, Maryland. Naval Institute Press, 1997.

McIntyre, Gene S., editor. *U.S. Navy Fleet Air Wing 7 Newsletters 1998-2001*, 2001.

Schoenfeld, Max. *Stalking the U-boat: U.S.A.A.F Offensive Antisubmarine Operations in World War II*. Washington and London: Smithsonian Institute Press, 1995.

Jarrett, M.J.M and Bernard Stevens. *U.S. Navy Fleet Air Wing 7 and the 479th Anti-Submarine Group U.S.A.A.F Dunkeswell 1943-1945*. Dunkeswell Memorial Museum, 1998.

Wolpert, Robet L. *The Story of One Eleven*. Emerson, NJ. Emerson Quality Press.

Government Sources

Navy Historical Center, Aviation History Branch, Navy Historical Center, Washington D. C. *Report on the mission of 12th August 1944 in which Lieutenant Joseph P. Kennedy Jr. lost his life*, 12 October 1997.

Naval Historical Center, Operational Archives Branch, Navy Historical Center. Washington, D.C. *Fleet Air Wing 7 War Diary March 1941-August 1945*.

Naval Historical Center, Operational Archives Branch, Navy Historical Center. Washington, D.C. *Fleet Air Wing Reports March 1941-August 1945*.

Navy Historical Center, Aviation History Branch, Washington, D.C. *VPB-103 War Diary 15 March 1943-1 31 August 1945*.

Naval Historical Center, Operational Archives Branch, Navy Historical Center. Washington, D.C. *VPB-105 War Diary 7 December 1941-27 June 1945*.

Navy Historical Center, Operational Archives Branch, Washington, D.C. *VPB-110 War Diary*, Microfiche No. 2982.

Navy Historical Center, Operational Archives Branch, Washington, D.C. *Fleet Air Wing-7 War Diary 1 March 1941-1 August 1945*.

Navy Historical Center, Operational Archives Branch, Washington, D.C. *Aircraft History Cards, Microfilm Reel 31*.

Navy Historical Center, Operational Archives Branch, Washington, D.C. *Aircraft History Cards, Microfilm Reel 35*.

Navy Historical Center, Operational Archives Branch, Washington, D.C. *Aircraft History Cards, Microfilm Reel 39*.

Navy Historical Center, Operational Archives Branch, Washington, D.C. *Aircraft History Cards, Microfilm Reel 46*.

Navy Historical Center, Operational Archives Branch, Washington, D.C. *Naval Aviation Safety Center Aircraft Accident Reports, Micro film Reel 25*.

Unpublished Sources

Jarrett, M.J.M. and Bernard Stevens. *Fleet Air Wing 7 Dunkeswell 1943-1945: 479th & U.S. Navy VB-103, VB-105, VB-107, VB-112, VB-110 & HEDRON 7, 2nd Issue*. Dunkeswell Memorial Museum, 2000.

Principal Projects Consultancy. Anti-Submarine Operations Centre Air Facility Dunkeswell U.S. Atlantic Fleet World War II. *Report on the Feasibility Study for the establishment of a permanent visitor experience*. Dunkeswell Airfield, Blackdown Hills, Devon, England, October 19.

Notes

1 M.J.M. Jarrett and Bernard Stevens, *U.S. Navy Fleet Air Wing 7 and 479ᵗʰ Anti-submarine Group U.S.A.A.F. Dunkeswell 1943-1945*, 2. The story originally appeared in Pullman's Weekly, June 6, 1962.

2 Greg Bade, *Navy Flyer Recalls WWII U-boat Attack*. Fleet Air Wing Seven Newsletters 2, no. 3 (July 1999). The original story appeared as an article from an unknown source.

3 George F. Poulos, *Fleet Air Wing Seven: Pioneer of Modern Antisubmarine Warfare*, Fleet Air Wing Seven Newsletters 1, no. 1.

4 M.J.M. Jarrett and Bernard Stevens, *The Battle of the Atlantic, Fleet Air Wing 7 Dunkeswell 1943-1945 479ᵗʰ U.S.A.A.F & U.S. Navy VB-103, VB-105, VB-107, VB-112, VB-110 & HEDRON-7*, 3.

5 The Mark-24 was also known as *Fido* and *Proctor*. See Mike Jarrett, *Mk-24 Acoustical Aerial Mine*, FAW-7 Newsletter 5 no. 2 (April 1, 2002). There is somewhat of a discrepency concerning which U-boat was lost. *The Dictionary of American Naval Aviation Squadrons: The History of VP, VPB, VP (HL) and VP (AM) Squadrons*, lists the U-640 while Paul Kemp's, *U-boats Destroyed: German Submarine Losses in the World Wars*, lists the U-657.

6 Admiral Ernest J. King, *Third and Final Report to the Secretary of the Navy Covering the Period 1 March 1945 to 1 October 1945*, dated 1 December 1945.

7 Schoenfeld, Max, *Stalking the U-boat: U.S.A.A.F Offensive Antisubmarine Operations in World War II*, 168.

8 Interview of Gene McIntrye by the author.

9 Information obtained through a U.S. government publication titled, *NAS Argentia*.

10 Interview with Gene McIntyre.

11 Charles P. Muckenthaler, Fleet Air Wing Seven Newsletters 4, no. 3 (July 1, 2001).

12 *Bombing Bond: Elkharten, German connect 54 years after World War II battle in the Atlantic*, Fleet Air Wing Seven News letters 1, no. 4, originally appeared as a newspaper article.

13 Charles P. Muckenthaler

14 Interview with Gene McIntyre.

15 See Fleet Air Wing 7 (FAW-7) War Diary. Historical information on FAW-7 Liberator squadrons was obtained through official U.S. Navy records on file at the Navy Historical Center, Washington, D.C., and the National Archives at College Park, Maryland. See Government Sources in the bibliography for additional information.

16 FAW-7 War Diary.

17 Memories from Bob Graham and Frank Kieper in Robert L. Wolpert's book *The Story of One Eleven*. Emerson Quality Press, 11-12.

18 Ibid.

19 Lt. Colonel "Buck" Cummings U.S.M.C. (Retired), *Page Knight Interview* (5 December 1997). The interview appeared in the Volume 4, Issue 2 of Fleet Air Wing Seven Newsletters 4, no. 2.

20 FAW-7 Diary.

21 Lt. Commander Paul Cory Salsbury U.S.N.R. (Retired), *The Fabulous Character*, Fleet Air Wing Seven Newsletters 2, no. 2. The original story appeared in a 1943 issue of Redbook Magazine written by Lt. (jg) Diver O. Jensen.

22 Loss of Wickstrom is attributed to either *Oberleutnant* Kurt Necesany or *Leutnant* Knud Gmelin. The V/KG40 was redesignated as the *I Gruppe/Zerstörergeschwader*. See Chris Gross, *Bloody Biscay*, 88.

23 Killed along with Blankenberg were *Oberfeldwebel* Bernhard Henrichs and *Unteroffizier* Otto Wawris, Goss, 231.

24 Letter from George Elbert to Gene S. McIntyre, *Fleet Air Wing Seven Newsletters* 1, no. 1.

25 Rear Admiral James R. Reedy U.S.N (Retired), *Submarines and Buzz Bombs*. Article from an unknown source appearing in Fleet Air Wing Seven Newsletters 1, no. 1.

26 FAW-7 War Diary, No. 19 Group Narrative, excerpts from log of FAW-7 Liaison Officer dated 23 November 1943.

27 Charles P. Muckenthaler, *Musings of Dunkeswell*, Fleet Air Wing Seven Newsletters 1, no. 3.

28 Letter from George Elbert to Gene S. McIntyre, *Fleet Air Wing Seven Newsletters* 1, no. 1.

29 Wolpert, 7.

30 Lt. Raymond L. North attacked a surfaced submarine on 24 October 1943.

31 Excerpts from the log of FAW-7 Liason Officer. NRS-1973-51, FAW-7 WWII Reports.

32 Paul Kemp, *U-boats Destroyed: German Submarine Losses in the World Wars*, 157.

33   Gunners involved were J.S. Cheney (AMM1c), J.F. Buehler (AOM3c), and J.E. Roche (AMM2c).

34   Felkel, Fred W. Jr., *Seven Days of Christmas in the Bay of Biscay.* Fleet Air Wing Seven Newsletters 1, no. 1.

35   Confidental dispatch 251650A from FAW-7 Diary.

36   Confidential dispatch 281402 from FAW-7 Diary.

37   Reedy identified the four fighters as HE-119-Es. However, that aircraft never went into production.

38   Muckenthaler, Charles P., , *Fleet Air Wing Seven Newsletters* 3, no. 4.

39   Fred W. Felkel Jr., *Seven Days of Christmas in the Bay of Biscay.* Fleet Air Wing Seven Newsletters 1, no. 1.

40   Charles Knauff, *A Day in the Life of Charley Knauff ACOM,* Fleet Air Wing Seven Newsletters 1, no. 4.

41   Francis "Red" Dean, *The Sinking of German U-Boat U-271,* Fleet Air Wing Seven Newsletters, January 2000.

42   Victoria Terrinoni, *World War II Days Remembered,* Minot Daily News, July 2, 2000.

43   Crew members *Feldwebel* Lothar Clemens and *Feldwebel* Werner Rueger were also killed, Goss 235.

44   Carlton L. Lillie, *Bay of Biscay Incident.* Fleet Air Wing Seven Newsletters 2, no. 1.

45   Also killed were *Obergefreiter* Georg Blach and *Feldwebel* Wilhelm Buxbaum, Goss, 235.

46   This was presumed as no wreckage or bodies were recovered.

47   See Goss, 248.

48   Excerpts from the log of FAW-7 Liason Officer. NRS-1973-51, FAW-7 WWII Reports.

49   Owen P. Windall, *Recollections of a Naval Liberator Pilot,* 5, 11. Appearing in Fleet Air Wing Seven Newsletters 3, no. 2.

50   Lt. Colonel "Buck" Cummings USMC (Retired), *Page Knight Interview* (5 December 1997). The interview appeared in the Volume 4, Issue 2 of Fleet Air Wing Seven Newsletters 4, no. 2.

51   FAW-7 War Diary.

52   Captain Don Higgins U.S.N. (Retired), *VB-114: Its life Away from FAW-7.* Fleet Air Wing Seven Newsletters 2, no. 2.

53   VB-105 After Action Report.

54   Rear Admiral James R. Reedy U.S.N (Retired), *Submarines and Buzz Bombs, Fleet Air Wing Seven Newsletters* 1, no. 1.

55   Willie Newsome, *Veteran reveals role in WWII secret Mission,* Orlando Sentinel, B-1, B-5.

56   Navy Historical Center, *Report on the mission of 12ᵗʰ August 1944 in which Lieutenant Joseph P. Kennedy Jr. lost his life.*

57   Fred Wake, *Firing on Fishing Boats.* Fleet Air Wing Seven Newsletters 3, no. 4.

58   Ralph M. Debevec, letter to the author.

59   James Alsop, *My Story,* Fleet Air Wing Seven Newsletters 2, no. 2.

60   U-boat successes by VB-107 were the U-598, 848, 849, 177, and 863.

61   Paul Kemp, *U-boats Destroyed,* 236-237.

62   See VB-103 After Action Report and James Alsop.

63   Mike Jarrett, E-mail to the author.

64   Ibid.

65   M.J.M. Jarrett and Bernard Stevens, *U.S. Navy Fleet Air Wing 7 and 479ᵗʰ Anti-submarine Group U.S.A.A.F. Dunkeswell 1943-1945,* 2. Also see *Anti-Submarine Operations Centre, Report on the Feasability Study for the establishment of a permanent visitor experience,* 1998.

66   Alsop.

67   Lisa Howard, *Dallas Jones is Speaker at Park Dedication to George A. Enloe,* Fleet Air Wing Seven Newsletters 1, no. 3. The story originally appeared in as a newspaper article.

68   Charly Knauff, *Post War Charley Knauff,* Fleet Air Wing Seven Newsletters 1, no. 3.

69   Lt. Colonel "Buck" Cummings USMC (Retired), *Page Knight Interview* (5 December 1997). The interview appeared in the Volume 4, Issue 2 of Fleet Air Wing Seven Newsletters 4, no. 2.

70   Gene S. McIntyre, *I thought you might want to know,* Fleet Air Wing Seven Newsletters 4, no. 4.

71   Belinda M. Paschal, *The 1 o'clock Train,* Fleet Air Wing Seven Newsletters 2, no. 3. The story originally appeared in the Antelope Valley Press August 11, 1995.

72   Bruce Lambert, *Charles Willis, Innovator in Aviation, Dies at 74.* Fleet Air Wing Seven Newsletters 2, no. 2. The obituary originally appeared in New York Times, March 21, 1993.

73   Owen P.Windall, *Recollections of a Naval Liberator Pilot,* 5, 11. Appearing in Fleet Air Wing Seven Newsletters 3, no. 2.

74   Mike Jarrett, E-mail to the author.

75   Mike Jarrett E-mail to the author.

Index